CHOOSING SIGNIFICANCE

Against The Odds

BRENT PHILLIPS

1415 South Voss ~ #110-399
Houston, TX 77057 ~ USA

NeverJustExist

Choosing Significance – Against the Odds
ISBN-13: 978-0988721203
ISBN-10: 0988721201
NeverJustExist
1415 South Voss #110-399
Houston, Texas 77549

DEDICATION

I dedicate this book to my mother, Maureen Phillips, the most significant person I know. This book is about choosing a life of significance, but you have *lived* a life of significance. Without your constant encouragement and example, this book would not exist. Your godly life has been a beacon, helping me navigate many storms and enabling me now to help others the way you have helped me.

I love you, Mom.

ACKNOWLEDGEMENTS

Daniela Phillips – Thank you, my precious wife, for your constant support, patience, and love in helping me accomplish a dream. "Behind every great man is an amazing woman."

Steve Woodrow – Thank you, Pastor, for entrusting me with the responsibility and the platform to preach the gospel and for the countless hours of prayer and support that birthed this message in me. Thank you for your example.

Clint Phillips – Thank you for giving me my first Bible study all those years ago and recognizing a gift in me that I did not see. Thank you for your support in ministry and for all the series we taught together.

Norma Jean – Thank you for helping compile and edit my materials that have now become this book. You are a sweetheart.

John Magee – Thank you for redesigning, producing and publishing this book for it's second printing. JohnMageeDesign.com

To everyone who prays and supports this ministry, thank you! I am sorry I don't have room to list you individually. Without God using you the way He does, this book would not exist.

CONTENTS

ENDNOTES

INTRODUCTION

Since as far back as I can remember, I wanted to make a difference. I wanted my life to count. I wanted to be part of the miracle that God was doing. Many people feel the same way, but they come to the ends of their lives having had little impact on those around them.

What is it that propels one person to press on against all odds to make a difference while another person stalls out and quits at the first sign of an obstacle or problem?

If you want to make a difference in your sphere of influence, what choices do you need to make? If you have been a quitter up to this point (and you want to change), what steps can you take to alter your life and become the one who can and will press on against the odds and make a difference?

Many of the answers to these questions are revealed through examining the life of an Old Testament man named Nehemiah. This common, ordinary, untrained person changed the course of history simply because he knew how to pray, how to connect with God, how to plan, and then how to act on his plan. He did all of this against huge odds.

In a time when the economy in his home city of Jerusalem was nonexistent and the threat of danger was continually lurking, he succeeded where others never even thought of trying. What was it that lifted this man from a place of obscurity to a place of strong leadership and equipped him to overcome various obstacles?

Travel back through time to learn amazing lessons from his timeless story. Learn from a history maker what it takes for each one of us to become a history maker.

CHAPTER 1

Significance is a Choice

CHAPTER 1: SIGNIFICANCE IS A CHOICE

Only a life lived for others is worth living.
– Einstein

We've all heard stories of those who, when the need required it, were gifted with superhuman strength or endurance. In nearly every case, such incidents involve someone choosing to help someone else.

Greater than Self

Many studies have shown that people who live for something greater than themselves accomplish, achieve, and survive against the odds. Consider this story:

A woman, named Lou Xiaoying, from the eastern Zhejiang province in China, found a newborn baby girl, who had been left to die in a trash can. Lou Xiaoying took the baby home, fed her, and raised her. Eventually this woman, who recycles rubbish to make a meager living, rescued more than thirty such abandoned babies.

She didn't appear to know or consider the odds against her. She didn't know she couldn't afford to feed and clothe that many children. After she was widowed and in her eighties, she didn't know she was too old to care for small children. All she knew was that she couldn't bear to let abandoned babies die.

As Christians, because of the price that Jesus paid for us, we too can live for something greater than ourselves. This is what Christianity is all about.

Changed in a Single Day

A man named Nehemiah, who lived thousands of years ago, can give us inspiration. He lived when the Israelites were in exile in Babylon. In the first chapter of the book of Nehemiah, we learn that this man led a comfortable life. In fact, he lived in the king's palace. He was the king's cupbearer; a simple job that required little or no training.

The main part of Nehemiah's job was to taste the king's wine before giving it to him, ensuring that no one had poisoned it. The two main requirements for the job were a high tolerance for risk and a good measure of trustworthiness. Obviously, one could hold this position only if he were completely trusted by the king. Every day, Nehemiah ran the risk of being poisoned.

Apart from that, his life was one of comfort, ease, and predictability. He brought the cup, tasted from it in view of the king, handed it to the king, and he was done. Presumably, the rest of the day he could lounge about the palace doing as he pleased.

One day, however, his life changed. He heard from some Jewish friends who had just returned from visiting the homeland. They said: "Those who survived the exile and are back in the province are in great trouble and disgrace. The wall of Jerusalem is broken down, and its gates have been burned with fire" (Nehemiah 1:3).

Selfless Prayer

This bad report moved Nehemiah to tears. He mourned and fasted for days, and then he prayed. The Bible records his selfless prayer:

Lord, the God of heaven, the great and awesome God, who keeps His covenant of love with those who love Him and keep His commandments, let your ear be attentive and your eyes open to hear the prayer your servant is praying before you day and night for your servants, the people of Israel. I confess the sins we Israelites, including myself and my father's family, have committed against you. We have acted very wickedly toward you. We have not obeyed the commands, decrees and laws you gave your servant Moses.

Remember the instruction you gave your servant Moses, saying, "If you are unfaithful, I will scatter you among the nations, but if you return to me and obey my commands, then even if your exiled people are at the farthest horizon, I will gather them from there and bring them to the place I have chosen as a dwelling for my Name."

They are your servants and your people, whom you redeemed by your great strength and your mighty hand. Lord, let your ear be attentive to the prayer of this your servant and to the prayer of your servants who delight in revering your name. Give your servant success today by granting him favor in the presence of this man. (Nehemiah 1:5–11)

In one short day, life was no longer so comfortable. He could not ignore the message nor could he forget it. He saw the need, and it brought him to his knees. It compelled him to pray and intercede for the city of Jerusalem.

Nehemiah was filled with compassion. He cared deeply for his people and his nation. Compassion is a powerful emotion. The power of God can flow out of compassion if we allow it. God's power that stems from compassion enables us to choose to go up against the odds and succeed. In the Gospels, we read how Jesus was moved by compassion to feed the multitudes, heal the sick, and raise the dead.

Why Overshadows How

You may have compassion in a certain area, for a certain person, or for a certain group of people. You want to help, you want to make a difference, but you wonder how. With your limited human reasoning, you see no way.

The *how* is not your part to figure out. Your part is to have a strong *why*. Why was Nehemiah so broken? Compassion for his fellow countrymen burned at the core of his being. That was his *why*. His reason why overshadowed all his questions about how.

In your life, you see things that need to be done. The reasons why God has placed a need in your heart are far more important than your knowing how to accomplish whatever needs to be done. When the *why* is in place, the *how* doesn't matter. You feel compelled to do something about that need. You are compelled to make a difference, even when it may seem that you cannot.

Nehemiah's compassion for those who were in need compelled him to make a choice to get involved, to do something incredible, and he changed history. His compassion enabled him to accomplish what was seemingly impossible.

Oftentimes we see a need that touches us deeply, but in the next moment we think up a dozen reasons why we can't do anything. It's all very well to want to help someone, but we've got our own issues we're struggling with. We're facing broken relationships, increasing debt, job problems, or health-related issues. The list goes on and on. How can we help someone else when we are facing giants of our own?

The truth is, the moment we take that first step to reach out and help someone else, our odds change. When you reach out to help another, your problems begin to diminish. At that moment, God becomes the deliverer of your situation. He will show you how.

"Don't be misled – you cannot mock the justice of God. You will always harvest what you plant. And let us not grow weary of doing good, for in due season we will reap, if we do not give up" (Galatians 6:7, 9 NLT).

Willing to Risk It All

Every day, Nehemiah laid his life on the line for the king while serving as cupbearer. After he made a choice to become involved in the need he saw, he set up a plan that would increase risk of his own death considerably. He planned to approach the king with a request. It may be difficult in our culture to grasp the sovereignty and power of the king, but if the king became displeased or even annoyed, he could order someone killed just for having the presumption of asking to speak to him. This tells us that Nehemiah was actually willing to risk it all, or die trying. His compassion led to commitment.

Are we like that? Or are we too comfortable? We have the status we've longed for; we've worked hard to get where we are and now we're just cruising. Are we willing to become like Nehemiah and risk it all for the sake of others?

If the needs of others aren't affecting our lives, if we have no concern for those outside of our immediate family, then there's a problem with our Christianity. If we can see people who are not saved and it doesn't bother us, it doesn't make us want to do something, then there's a problem with our Christianity.

Jesus' commanded us to "Go into all the world and preach the gospel" (Mark 16:15). He said, "You are the light of the world" (Matthew 5:14), and "If anyone has this world's wealth and sees that his brother man is in need, and yet hardens his heart against him—how can such a one continue to love God?" (1 John 3:17).

Choosing Significance

Nehemiah, as cupbearer, would not have been considered by others to be significant. He could have lived his entire life, died an old man, and no one would have known his name or even that he existed. But he became significant with his choice to get involved. What significant impact are we having on those around us? Are people impacted in a positive way because of our presence? Our work? Our involvement? Our input? Our love?

If someone is in danger and escapes from that imminent danger, we call that person a *survivor*. If someone saves the life of another, we call that person a *rescuer*. Each one of us is called to be a rescuer.

In the movie *Titanic*, as the ship sinks completely under the water, the camera pulls out, showing the half-filled lifeboats rowing away from the sinking ship. People are thrashing about in the freezing waters, screaming for help; yet, the people in the lifeboats row away from them. They refuse to help, fearing for their own safety. If you remember watching that scene, how did you feel? Shocked? Revolted? Disgusted?

If you think you would never do something like that, think again. Jesus is our lifeboat, and many Christians are in the boat all alone. The charge given to us by Jesus is to get as many people as we can to fill our boats. Many of us are afraid to get a little wet or cold for the sake of rescuing others. Many Christians just want to row their boats to safety and not be bothered or inconvenienced.

We can all think of reasons why impact, change, liberation, and significance can be left for someone else. Someone else will do it. Someone else has better qualifications. Someone else has more time. Someone else knows how to take care of that problem. We see injustice and suffering all around us, and the way we make ourselves feel better is by telling ourselves that someone else will do it. What can I do? I'm insignificant.

Making a Difference

While walking along a beach, an elderly gentleman saw someone in the distance lean down, pick up something, and throw it into the ocean.

As the old man got closer, he noticed the figure was a young man. He was picking up starfish one by one and tossing each one gently back into the water.

"Good morning!" the old man yelled. "May I ask what it is that you're doing?"

The young man paused, looked up, and replied, "Throwing starfish back into the ocean."

The old man smiled, and said, "I must ask, why are you throwing starfish into the ocean?"

"The sun is up and the tide is going out," the young man said. "If I don't throw them in, they'll die."

"But, young man, do you not realize that there are miles and miles of beach and there are starfish all along every mile? You can't possibly make a difference!"

The young man listened politely. Then he bent down, picked up another starfish, and threw it into the ocean. He said, "It made a difference for that one."

If we believe we *are* insignificant, then we will remain insignificant. The moment we decide to act, however, we become significant in the life of another. We can make a difference with that one.

The walls of Jerusalem had been in ruins for more than one hundred years before the news reached Nehemiah. What made Nehemiah believe that a lowly cupbearer could bring about a change, a change that entire generations before him could not achieve?

Because God Loves You

For every negative thought you may have about yourself and your own limitations, the Scripture has a truth to refute it. Romans 8 lists a bunch of difficulties and then asks, "What, then, shall we say in response to these things? If God is for us, who can be against us?" (v. 31).

Your life will become significant when you choose to believe God's Word, step out, and take action. A violin is an instrument and cannot be anything else, but the beauty and purpose of a violin is only experienced when it is played. A violin was not made to remain in its case but to be used and played. You are significant because God loves you, but just like the violin, your significance and purpose can only be experienced as you give to others.

This brings to mind a poem:

> 'Twas battered and scarred,
> And the auctioneer thought it
> hardly worth his while
> To waste his time on the old violin,
> but he held it up with a smile.

"What am I bid, good people", he cried,
"Who starts the bidding for me?"
"One dollar, one dollar, Do I hear two?"
"Two dollars, who makes it three?"
"Three dollars once, three dollars twice, going for three,"

But, No,
From the room far back a gray bearded man
Came forward and picked up the bow,
Then wiping the dust from the old violin
And tightening up the strings,
He played a melody, pure and sweet
As sweet as the angel sings.

The music ceased and the auctioneer
With a voice that was quiet and low,
Said "What now am I bid for this old violin?"
As he held it aloft with its bow.

"One thousand, one thousand, Do I hear two?"
"Two thousand, Who makes it three?"
"Three thousand once, three thousand twice,
Going and gone," said he.

The audience cheered,
But some of them cried,
"We just don't understand."
"What changed its worth?"
Swift came the reply.
"The Touch of the Master's Hand."

"And many a man with life out of tune
All battered and bruised with hardship
Is auctioned cheap to a thoughtless crowd
Much like that old violin

A mess of pottage, a glass of wine,
A game and he travels on.
He is going once, he is going twice,
He is going and almost gone.

But the Master comes,
And the foolish crowd never can quite understand,
The worth of a soul and the change that is wrought
By the Touch of the Master's Hand.
– Myra Brooks Welch

Sometimes we pray for God to speak to us and lead us, and then we wait for the clouds to part, lightning to come down, and God to speak in a loud voice. That could happen. Much more often, God speaks by giving us a thought, a sense of something deep within our heart. We feel troubled over a need that no one else seems to see or care about. We may say, "God, I want to make a difference in my world," but then we fail to choose action. We sit back and do nothing.

Nehemiah expected God to do something through him. The Bible never records that he prayed and then sat around wondering if God cared enough to answer or send someone to fix the problem. Nehemiah simply assumed that his God was merciful, faithful, and forgiving. Long before this moment, Nehemiah already had a strong relationship with God. He simply turned to God in faith, praying for the power of God to do something historic. At the same time, he believed he could do something historic because of God's power.

The Bible contains thousands of promises for those who trust in God, and not one of those promises requires that your circumstances be favorable for the promises to come to pass. In fact, God's promises are most valuable in hopeless situations. God's light shines the brightest in the darkest of situations.

Choose to Become Significant

What makes you significant to God is His love for you, but what makes you significant to others is God's love *through you.*

The way to become significant is to *choose* to become significant. God presents choices to you, but the choice is yours. It's God's will that none perish and go to hell, but people are going to hell every day. It's our choice to make a difference by showing them the way to eternal life.

God says that if we draw close to Him, He will draw close to us (James 4:8). That means we can be as close to God as we choose to be. In spite of that promise, most people choose to stray far from God's presence.

The same applies to being significant. It's not God's will that we go idly through life. We wake up, go to work, go home, do a few chores, watch a little TV, go to bed, get up, and do it all over again. That's hardly a significant life.

Every single one of us was born to be significant; to be a history maker – but it's a choice. Here's a simple definition of the significant life: *Because you are alive, someone's world is different in a positive way.* Just because you showed up, someone's life is improved.

Solutions Come through Christ

When you see a problem, you are the one who can make a difference. When Jesus showed up on the scene and saw a need, He did not say, "Sorry, but you'll have to ask someone else." On the contrary, Jesus was always the solution to the problem.

As Christians, because Christ dwells in us, when someone is hurting or in need and we show up on the scene – guess who just showed up? Jesus! The solution just showed up.

When someone is sick and we show up, the solution just showed up. No more looking around for someone else. No more waiting. No more hedging. When someone is in need, you'll be the one to say, "Yes, I'll pray for you."

Remember the story in the Bible of the Good Samaritan in Luke 10:25–37? The two religious leaders passed by a man who was lying injured by the side of the road. I'm sure their minds were filled with a million reasons why they could not (would not) stop and help. Will we be like those two who passed by; or will we be like the Samaritan who, even though he was despised by the Jews, stopped and helped? Was this "impure" Samaritan's life significant? Ask the man whose life he saved.

Think of the people in your life who have been significant in ways both large and small. What would your life be like without them? Perhaps an individual believed in you and encouraged you when no one else seemed to care. What were that person's qualifications? Rich? Famous? Well trained? Or was that person qualified simply because he or she reached out to you in your need? You can do the same thing.

Remember the woman in China who saved the abandoned babies she found in the rubbish heap. For years, no one knew she existed. Only within the past few years did word get out about her life of giving. By caring for others, she lived a life of significance.

Each day, keep your eyes and ears open to those who are in need of an encouraging word, a helping hand, a hug, or even just a smile. Remember, your life becomes significant when you choose to affect the life of another in a positive way.

Reflection Questions

1. When was the last time you were moved to your knees for the sake of others?
2. How do Christians shine God's light? How can we shine with the resources and blessings we have been given?
3. Who in your life right now is waiting for God to use you to be the miracle?

It takes great courage to faithfully follow what we know to be true.
– Sara E. Anderson

Significance through Prayer

CHAPTER 2:
SIGNIFICANCE THROUGH PRAYER

A man is powerful on his knees.
– Corrie Ten Boom

When Nehemiah learned that Jerusalem was in ruins, he also learned that the city walls had been torn down and the wooden gates had been burned. This meant the people living in the city were in constant danger from attack by invaders and wild animals.

Nehemiah was crushed to think that God's city was in such a condition. This was the city where the temple of Solomon had been built and where the Spirit of the living God had once resided in all His glory. Now it lay desolate.

What did Nehemiah do next? Did he cry for a few days and then go on with his life? Did he gather a few friends, put together a few supplies, and race off toward Jerusalem? We've all been guilty of doing one extreme or the other. We can be all gung ho, fired up, and ready to serve God, but then run out of steam and give up. The other extreme is, we move out in our own power and intellect, leaving God in the dust. Often, our actions aren't in line with God's plans.

Prayer and Fasting

Wisely, Nehemiah turned to God by praying and fasting. He spent many days in God's presence, asking, seeking, and listening. His heart was open. He was positioned to receive explicit instructions from God, and he asked God to give him special favor with the king.

Once his heart was prepared, Nehemiah appeared before King Artaxerxes. Upon seeing Nehemiah, the king commented about his servant's sad countenance. "Why does your face look so sad when you are not ill? This can be nothing but sadness of heart" (Nehemiah 2:2). The king's remark tells us that Nehemiah had always been an upbeat, cheerful person. When the king asked Nehemiah why he was sad, it provided the perfect opportunity to speak about his grief over Jerusalem being in ruins.

Upon hearing the story, the king asked an amazing question. Keep in mind, this is the ruler over a vast kingdom wherein he is in control of many peoples, lands, and great wealth. He very simply asked Nehemiah, "What do you *want?*" This king, this powerful ruler, asked his own servant, "What do you want?" A profound moment.

Nehemiah's Audacity

Did Nehemiah stammer, stutter, and choke? Not at all. Because he had been in continual prayer, he was confident that God was on the scene. He had his answer ready, because he already had a plan.

This servant, this slave, if you will, put in for a *leave of absence.* Such audacity! "If it pleases the king and if your servant has found favor in his sight, let him send me to the city in Judah where my ancestors are buried so that I can rebuild it" (Nehemiah 2:5).

Next, the king asked his servant how long a leave of absence he would need, so Nehemiah gave him a time. He must have already considered that question to have such a quick answer. By now, as the two are chatting away, it's pretty clear that Nehemiah has great favor.

While things are going his way, Nehemiah takes the opportunity to present a list of all he needs for the journey. Again, remember that he's not flying by the seat of his pants here. Nehemiah has heard from God and knows *exactly* what he needs that the king can provide:
  • Letters to the governors of Trans-Euphrates so Nehemiah and his fellow travelers will have safe conduct.
  • A letter to Asaph, keeper of the royal park, so he will provide timber to make beams for the gates and for the city wall and for the residence *I will occupy.*

Notice that Nehemiah had the presence of mind to ask for enough lumber to rebuild the city wall, but also a little extra for a house of his own. Again, imagine the audacity.

Not only does Nehemiah get the needed letters and the timber, but the king generously sends along his own army officers and cavalry!

No Talent Required

Now picture this scene with the lowly cupbearer in the role of leader of an entourage traveling from Shushan (in modern-day Iran) to Jerusalem, Israel, accompanied by the king's handpicked soldiers, followed by carts filled with the best of the king's timber.

Let's think about this. Could there have been someone actually living in the city of Jerusalem who knew more about construction and building than Nehemiah? He had spent years serving wine to the king. How much could he know about building?

Could there have been someone in Jerusalem with more leadership ability? Someone who knew the place better and was well connected? Someone who had more resources? We see no evidence of Nehemiah asking these kinds of questions.

So many times in our culture, we tend to be in awe of talent. We are captivated by people who have amazing talents or gifts but little in the way of character. It could be a sports celebrity or a famous star in the entertainment industry. We allow these highly revered public figures to diminish how we perceive our own abilities. Talent by itself is not always what God is looking for. God has all the ability He needs; what He is looking for is availability and a heart that will trust in Him.

The Bible Study

Many years ago, while my brother, Clint, was attending university in South Africa, he and another Christian friend, Mike, from his rugby team, were concerned about their team members. They played rugby four times a week with fifteen guys whom they cared about. They knew if their teammates' lives ended suddenly, they would not go to heaven because Jesus was not Lord of their lives. What could they do?

The Lord didn't tell my brother in a mighty voice to start a Bible study, nor did anyone approach them at church with a prophecy saying, "The Lord is going to use you to start a Bible study." But Clint and Mike knew they had to do *something*.

As the two began to pray about it, they came across a six-week course called "Athletes in Action." All they had to do was read four pages, and they could have a Bible study. They didn't have to come up with anything on their own. They could give everybody a booklet and then read four pages together. That was the start. It didn't sound difficult.

Once you take that first step, however, you often find out that you need more prayer, because the next step looks even more challenging. Their next step was to invite fifteen unbelievers from their rugby team to attend their

Bible study. To say they were nervous would be an understatement. They didn't even call it a Bible study, because if they had, their teammates wouldn't have listened to the rest of the sentence before saying, "No, thank you."

Their invitation went something like this: "Uh, listen. Mike and I are going to start a, uh, *a group*. We're going to talk about sports and talent and (whisper) *God,* and other important things in life that could help all of us to become better sportsmen." Some of the guys picked up on the church thing and turned them down flat. But a few agreed to attend.

At the first meeting, four guys showed up. They read through the material. Although nothing spectacular happened, my brother was filled with excitement. He realized he had just moved into the land of significance by affecting the lives of others. The journey had begun with one small step of obedience.

The next week, even though only three guys came, they were still excited. One of the guys underlined something in his study book and another actually asked a question and a short discussion ensued. They were off to the races.

On the third week, however, only two guys showed up. Discouragement started to set in. Clint and Mike had to fight thoughts that many people face when choosing a life of significance: *This is never going to work. This is going nowhere. No one wants to come to a Bible study every week.*

All through the weeks, they continued to pray. "Lord, this is for You; we're just being obedient. We don't know how to do this stuff. All we know is that we have to do something. Lord, we'd love for someone else to do this. We'd love for some good speaker to come in and help. Or someone who knows more about the Bible than we do. Or perhaps a really famous rugby player – that would get their attention. So, Lord, if there's someone else, please bring them along. In the meantime, we'll just keep trudging away."

Exponential Growth

The Lord blessed their feeble attempts. Before they knew it, they had half the team attending. Soon guys asked, "Can we bring our girlfriends?" "Can I invite a friend who is not on the rugby team?" The day arrived when they had so many people they had to create two separate Bible studies. Within a few months, those two Bible studies became so full of people meeting together, praying, and studying God's Word that they split into *five*

Bible studies. By this time, my brother wasn't simply leading a Bible study. He had become a leader of leaders.

Nobody had ever told my brother that he was a great leader or that he had leadership qualities. When you choose to be significant, even if you're bumbling your way around while praying and trusting God, things will start to happen.

Once the Bible study opened to anyone, rather than just team members, I began to attend. As studies grew, Clint approached me about leading one of the groups. Now Clint's obedience extended into my life and forever changed me. These Bible studies helped start my ministry simply because I was given an opportunity to lead.

No one had ever primed my brother or me for ministry through teaching and preaching. No one had ever told us it was our gifting or calling. We had helped several years in our church's children's ministry, but that's hardly a prerequisite to minister to a bunch of tough rugby players. Clint and I were normal Christians; we attended church every week and occasionally invited someone to come with us. No one could have accused us of being the evangelistic type. But all of that changed. We began to live lives of significance.

As our friends who attended these Bible studies started moving away, our impact moved with them. Today, there are hundreds of Bible studies all around the globe because of two ill-equipped rugby players (and one equally ill-equipped younger brother) who cared enough to do something and trusted God to help them against the odds.

Action Required

My brother had compassion on his teammates and was concerned about where they would spend eternity. Compassion, however, is not enough. Action is required.

Imagine if your youngster is playing outside and he falls and skins his knee. He runs into the house crying and you take a look. It's raw and bleeding and looks to be pretty painful. Your compassion kicks in and you say, "Aw, that's terrible that you hurt yourself. I'm so sorry. Poor you. I bet that really hurts."

Your son is crying harder and now a bit of panic sets in because of the blood. "It's bleeding! Can't you see?" "Yes, I know and my heart is breaking for you."

Here we have awareness and compassion, but no action. No follow up. Compassion must be coupled with action. What's called for here is for the scrape to be cleaned, the antiseptic applied, and a bandage fixed in place – not to mention a warm hug.

Were there more qualified people to start a Bible study than Clint and his buddy Mike? Absolutely. But looking back, I'm thankful they didn't disqualify themselves.

Within Your Reach

What little thing could you do in obedience to God? Pray and ask Him to show you. Perhaps you could invite a coworker to church. Perhaps you could offer to pray for someone who is ill or spend time with someone who is young in the Lord and needs instruction or encouragement. It's been said that you can count the seeds in one apple, but only God knows how many apples reside in one single seed! What is it that lies within you waiting to be born?

Often the sign of where our greatest significance will be is in what moves us, what stirs us, or grieves us. Nehemiah was grieved by the plight of Jerusalem and its people.

Living a life of significance begins with spending time in prayer, seeking guidance and direction. Before Jesus selected His twelve disciples, He spent an entire night in prayer. I find that to be amazing. If the Son of God needed a night of prayer before making this crucial decision, how much more do we need to be people of prayer?

Before ever approaching King Artaxerxes, Nehemiah spent four months in fasting and prayer. When the moment came to reveal his plan to the king, Nehemiah was ready. Never forget that prayer is an essential part of living a life of significance.

Reflection Questions

1. Are you more of a procrastinator or a gung ho person when you see a need?
2. What kinds of things or people or needs move you, stir you, or grieve you?
3. Are you using the gift of prayer to prepare your path before you set your foot on it? If not, what will you do to change?

CHAPTER 3
Dealing with Difficult People

CHAPTER 3:
DEALING WITH DIFFICULT PEOPLE

If you are going through hell, keep going.
— Winston Churchill

When Nehemiah appeared on the scene to improve the demolished city of Jerusalem, not everyone was happy to see him. In fact, he was met with almost instant opposition from multiple groups and circumstances.

Opposition from Leaders

Three powerful leaders were angry. The Bible says they "were very much disturbed that someone had come to promote the welfare of the Israelites." (Nehemiah 2:10). They were especially upset that King Artaxerxes had set Nehemiah in the office of governor of Judah.

The three leaders were Sanballat the Hononite, Tobiah the Ammonite official, and Geshem the Arab. Sanballat served as the governor of Samaria, and it's probable that Nehemiah would never have gotten past him had it not been for Nehemiah's letter from King Artaxerxes. These three men exerted a great deal of influence in the region. Geographically, Judah was surrounded on three sides by their opposition.

Besides the opposition from these three leaders, Nehemiah sensed other difficulties. Under the cover of darkness, Nehemiah took it upon himself to make an inspection tour around the entire city. Wisely, he didn't want anyone to know what he was doing – not his enemies nor his countrymen. This was also obviously his prayer time, because God was giving him a carefully detailed rebuilding program.

Opposition from Random People

Nehemiah faced opposition caused by the people he came to help. In our Christian walk, we often feel as though we're battling against people. Many times spiritual warfare wears the face of someone close to us. It may be your boss, your spouse, other family members, coworkers, and, sadly, sometimes those in your church. It can even be the very people you are trying to help! If we're not careful, we will be tempted to make that person into the enemy, but that person is not the enemy.

These people are just difficult people, and we need to learn to deal with them. The things that have caused me the most pain, the most setbacks, the most stumbling blocks, have never been difficult circumstances. People have always been the biggest problem. Can you relate? Often it is the people we least expect who do the most damage or cause the most hurt.

Listening to the Holy Spirit

If we are going to succeed against the odds, we need to know who to listen to, who to sidestep, who to tell to simmer down, and who to ignore. How will we know this? Only by the help of the Holy Spirit. By listening to God's wisdom, we will learn.

Did you know that people can even use Scripture to lure you off course and prevent you from succeeding against all odds and living a life of significance? Satan tried this tactic with Jesus, twisting Scripture in an attempt to take him off course. (Matthew 4:1–11)

Do you know how to cook a crab? When you cook a crab, you must place it in a pot with several other crabs. If one crab is in the pot alone, it will crawl out. But if you put several in the pot at once, every time one tries to crawl out, the other crabs pull it down again.

Have you ever experienced this? You're in a group of friends and God starts doing something exciting in your life. You're being set free, and all of a sudden the people who you thought were your friends, the people you thought would be the most excited for you, start to turn on you. Why? Because you're starting to climb out of the pot. When you decide to make a difference and stop just existing, you shine a light that makes people who are coasting feel uncomfortable.

When you decide to go against the odds, you can count on it that not everyone will be excited for you. A person you used to think had your back may all of a sudden stick a knife in it instead.

We must learn how to get over people. The person who hurt you, the person who turned on you is not your enemy. Ephesians 6:12 explains it this way: "For our struggle is not against flesh and blood, but against the rulers, against the authorities, against the powers of this dark world and against the spiritual forces of evil in the heavenly realms." If we cannot recognize the true enemy, we can find ourselves fighting against God Himself.

Discerning the Fires

A related problem we must learn about is which fires to put out and which fires to leave alone. If we don't learn this lesson, we'll never get to the place where God wants us to be. We'll never be able to go against the odds because the devil will keep us dancing around, dealing with little fires here and little fires there. Much valuable time will slip away, and we will fail to accomplish what God has designed for us to accomplish. Here's an example in my own life.

I was the new pastor in a certain church. The Monday after I had preached for the second time, an article appeared in the local newspaper. The article announced that I was being sued for $250,000 because of my computer hacking. One angry lady wrote to the newspaper stating that scam artists like me should never be allowed to preach and that the church should remove me.

Up until that Monday, few people knew my name, but now I was the "hot" news. That accusation was terrible, and I desperately wanted to put out the fire. I wanted to defend myself and call out, "It's not true! It's not true! None of it is true! How can they say that about me?"

I was in turmoil, casting about for what to do. Every idea had its set of possible repercussions. Believe me, one of the best ways the devil gets us off course is by lighting a blazing fire. While we're busy putting it out, he's in another direction, lighting a new one. Now the next blaze must be extinguished. The pattern is never ending. He keeps us busy trying to defend our character. This is why it's imperative that we know when to put the fire out and when to let the fire burn.

In seeking a plan, I sought the Lord. What happened with the newspaper article? I never had to put out that fire; I let it burn itself out. In the end, the Lord vindicated me and promoted me. A subsequent newspaper article came out, describing the situation as a modern-day David and Goliath story and implying I was David. I never had to put out that fire, but I did need the mind of God to know what to do and not to do.

If we want to live a life of significance, we can expect the devil to light fires. For those of us who trust the Lord, He can use those fires to light our pathway to victory. God uses people to accomplish His purposes. The devil will use people to hinder God's purposes. Wisdom is knowing the difference.

Jesus clearly instructs us to "bless those who curse you, pray for those who mistreat you" (Luke 6:28). When we face opposition, we are called to pray for our opponents.

Likely, we can all recall times we faced opposition. A more searching question is whether we have ever been the one the devil has used to spark the fire and cause the opposition. Each one of us can be used by the enemy if we're not careful. You're tired. You're irritable. You're discouraged. You got offended. And, then, you lashed out and offended someone.

The devil loves to use Christian brothers and sisters against one another, because it's the area where it's least expected. Often it's the area where it hurts the most. But when we consistently commit our ways to God, the devil has a much bigger challenge if he tries to use us. When we pray, when we're full of the Holy Spirit, there's no room for the devil. The sign says, "No Vacancy." He has to flee.

Facing Ridicule

We have already noted that Nehemiah diligently spent hours in prayer before he approached the king regarding his plans to rebuild the walls of Jerusalem. He saw it all in his mind's eye. He envisioned the walls being completely repaired and rebuilt. He was determined, convinced, and committed. He knew he wasn't doing the work in his strength but was totally leaning on God.

One of the first weapons the enemy used against Nehemiah was ridicule. The three leaders scoffed at the very idea of the walls being rebuilt.

But when Sanballat the Horonite, Tobiah the Ammonite official and Geshem the Arab heard about it, they mocked and ridiculed us. "What is this you are doing?" they asked. "Are you rebelling against the king?"(Nehemiah 2:19)

"What are those feeble Jews doing? Will they restore their wall? Will they offer sacrifices? Will they finish in a day? Can they bring the stones back to life from those heaps of rubble – burned as they are?"

Tobiah the Ammonite, who was at his side, said, "What they are building – even a fox climbing up on it would break down their wall of stones!" (Nehemiah 4:2–3)

When you step out to do something significant for God, you may be mocked and ridiculed as Nehemiah was. Why? It's because you're disrupting the mockers' comfort levels. When you speak out and say, "I'm going all out for God," not everyone in the church will be excited about your declaration.

Perhaps in your Bible study, you say, "I think we could be experiencing God in a much greater dimension than we are now." Not everyone will agree with you. Again, you're making them feel uncomfortable, and people can react strangely when they feel discomfort.

Did you know that evangelist and Bible teacher Joyce Meyer was once asked to leave the church where she attended? At that time, she had not one friend who believed in her calling. She never stopped; she never slowed down. Today, millions of people around the world listen to her teaching and have been powerfully affected in their Christian walk by this sixty-nine-year-old woman.

This is why it's essential to be led by the Lord, just as Nehemiah was. Before we share our pearls with others, we have to have a solid, concrete foundation in knowing what God says and what He has called us to do in response through His power. Once that's established, then the ridicule may come but it cannot shake our foundation.

Fighting Threats

Once Nehemiah's enemies realized that ridicule had no effect, they brought out their next weapon: threats. "But when Sanballat, Tobiah, the Arabs, the Ammonites and the people of Ashdod heard that the repairs to Jerusalem's walls had gone ahead and that the gaps were being closed, they were very angry. They all plotted together to come and fight against Jerusalem and stir up trouble against it." (Nehemiah 4:7–8)

Now things were getting serious. The enemy loves to use fear to demoralize the saints of God. Threats are nothing more than instigators of fear, the real enemy, because fear is where the devil's power resides. In the opposite realm, faith is where God's power resides. When we exercise faith, God can do the impossible on our behalf. But fear brings down the mightiest of people. Fear gives the devil a foothold. So why does he come with threats? To try to shake us up, to try to bring fear, to make us quit!

I once read an article that explained how a bear flushes his prey from its hiding place. When a bear has lost the prey's scent and can't locate it, he begins to growl and thrash about, charging in all directions. Now the prey, perhaps a deer, doesn't realize it is completely hidden and safe. From the noise the deer hears, it fears the bear is charging right at it. So what does it do? The worst thing possible: It comes out of hiding by running away. Now the chase is on, and the deer is apt to lose.

In the same way, we can be hidden with Christ in God (Colossians 3:3), and dwell in the secret place of the most high God (Psalm 91:1). Then the enemy comes at us as a roaring lion and we begin to speak our fears, doubts, and unbelief. We tell the devil exactly how we're feeling, and now we're caught.

God has given you a purpose, plan, or idea. You've seen a need, and you're ready to go after it. You've prayed and God said, "Yes, I will empower you to do this." All of a sudden a threat comes. What do you do? You are attempted to think, *Maybe God was confused. Maybe I missed God. I love God, but not at this price.*

If you stand your ground, it may cost you friends, family relationships, position, and more. Are you willing to go on irrespective of threats?

"Truly I tell you," Jesus replied, "no one who has left home or brothers or sisters or mother or father or children or fields for me and the gospel will fail to receive a hundred times as much in this present age: homes, brothers, sisters, mothers, children and fields – along with persecutions – and in the age to come eternal life" (Mark 10:29–30).

Dealing with Discouragement

Nehemiah didn't seem too surprised by opposition from the enemy leaders round about him, but when his own people began to waver, it appeared much more devastating. The people in Judah said, "The strength of the laborers is giving out, and there is so much rubble that we cannot rebuild the wall" (Nehemiah 4:10).

"We cannot." His own people spoke these words. Those who would have benefitted most from having a solid wall built around the city; those who had lived with the danger of no protection. Now the answer to their dilemma lay before them; the path was open. Their response is, "We cannot!"

Discouragement had infiltrated the people. That's how it will be with us. The very people we counted on, the ones we thought shared our vision, will start to feel discouraged and begin to jump ship – or worse yet, turn on us. All of a sudden, our world begins to shake, and we can be infected by their feelings. Discouragement can come from the people we trust the most; those to whom we have given our hearts. They're the ones who can do the most damage.

The discouraging words that Nehemiah heard did not deter him. The vision and the call were deeply imbedded in his heart, and he knew his vision was coming to fruition. He didn't waste words, replying to their remarks. Instead, he chose to get busy, organizing the people into efficient, effective work teams.

Being Kicked Out of Church

During my first year in Aspen, Colorado, after much prayer, I received my first call to ministry. I experienced a passion and a yearning that I had never felt before. I sensed a need to launch a service for young people my age, since the church I attended offered nothing for that age group.

Excited to have received a clear call from God, I couldn't wait to get started. This church had only about seven people who attended regularly. I chose it because I longed to help make an impact.

First, I spent time in faithful service to the pastor to demonstrate my character. I waited for the right time before sharing my idea with him, which was to launch a Sunday evening service. When I felt the timing was right, I approached him, making my request. He agreed to let me start a service on Sunday evenings. My brother Clint was there also, and he agreed to help, along with a deacon named Curt. The three of us did all the work: setting up, taking an offering, leading worship, and preaching. We did not want to become a burden on the pastor. Our goal was to come alongside to help.

God began to move in an amazing way. After only a few weeks, more than thirty people were in attendance. This was unheard of for this small church.

But, much like Nehemiah's experience, not everyone was excited. The pastor, we quickly discovered, was furious. Because the Sunday morning service still had only seven people, it made him look bad, in his own eyes at least.

What happened? We ended up getting kicked out of the church. We were incredulous. The discouragement I experienced was overwhelming.

Questions swirled in my mind. *How could this have happened when all I wanted to do was make a difference? How could one jealous man ruin an entire ministry?* I thought it was all over for me; I'd been disgraced.

In hindsight, I could have spared myself a great deal of heartache, discouragement, and wasted energy if I had been firmly aligned with God's plan – like Nehemiah. Obviously, my ministry didn't end that day. On the contrary, that setback provided the starting block of a ministry that now reaches around the globe.

Ignoring Distractions

When Nehemiah's enemies saw how fast the work on the wall was progressing, they resorted to a new tactic. Ridicule didn't work. Threats didn't work. Discouragement didn't work, so their next weapon was distraction.

> *When word came to Sanballat, Tobiah, Geshem the Arab and the rest of our enemies that I had rebuilt the wall and not a gap was left in it – though up to that time I had not set the doors in the gates – Sanballat and Geshem sent me this message: "Come, let us meet together in one of the villages on the plain of Ono."*
>
> *But they were scheming to harm me; so I sent messengers to them with this reply: "I am carrying on a great project and cannot go down. Why should the work stop while I leave it and go down to you?" Four times they sent me the same message, and each time I gave them the same answer.*
>
> *Then, the fifth time, Sanballat sent his aide to me with the same message, and in his hand was an unsealed letter in which was written:*
>
> *"It is reported among the nations – and Geshem says it is true – that you and the Jews are plotting to revolt, and therefore you are building the wall. Moreover, according to these reports you are about to become their king and have even appointed prophets to make this proclamation about you in Jerusalem: 'There is a king in Judah!' Now this report will get back to the king; so come, let us meet together."* (Nehemiah 6:1–4)

Over and over again, Sanballat tried to coerce Nehemiah into meeting with him outside the protection of the city. On the surface, it sounded great.

His enemies appeared ready to become peaceful; they were ready to talk things out. Perhaps this was the answer to their problems – a nice, peaceful sit-down meeting.

Nehemiah never yielded to their distractions. Even when the letter arrived accusing him of revolting against the king, he did not yield. His mind, his focus, was fixed.

This is reminiscent of the story of Joseph in Genesis. God showed Joseph in dreams that he would one day become a great leader and that his family members would bow down to him. In response, his brothers, who came to hate him, sold him into slavery.

Throughout his young life, Joseph never let go of his dream. Even when he was unjustly placed in prison, he served God and rose to a place of leadership within the prison. By anyone's standards, Joseph had every right to be angry, bitter, and resentful. He chose the better way; he chose God's way.

Prison seemed a long, long way from his dreams, but one day he was promoted from the prison to the palace. And his family eventually did bow down to him. God's plan for Joseph came to fruition because Joseph never let himself be distracted from what he knew was God's plan.

Letting Go

God has given each one of us dreams and desires; some of them are so big they seem impossible. Along the way, some of us have let go of those dreams because of ridicule, discouragement, threats, and distraction. Joseph is proof that when we place our lives in God's hand, no circumstance or person can stop us from achieving our dreams – even against all odds. No one can stop you from being significant when you let God build that image inside you and you hold onto His power.

"All things work together for good for those who love God and are called according to His purpose" (Romans 8:28). "All things" means all the junk, all the mess, from your past whether you caused your own problems or you were the victim. It's time to stop blaming others. It's time to release the anger, bitterness, and resentment. It's time to get over people and move forward.

To move forward, you can choose to say, "Lord, I'm committed to leading a life of significance starting today. It doesn't matter what has happened in my past. You're big enough to reconstruct whatever it is I need."

Once you make that commitment, it's time to pick up and dust off the dreams that you left behind all those years ago. God gave you those dreams in the first place. He wants to use you to become significant in His kingdom.

Reflection Questions

1. Can you recall a situation when the devil used someone to hinder you? How did you respond?
2. Was there a time when the devil used you or attempted to use you to light a fire, hindering another person's desire or ministry?
3. What fires are you facing now that threaten to burn up everything you are trying to accomplish?
4. What setbacks have seemed debilitating at the time but later turned out for the good, for you or for someone else?
5. What dreams have died because of your prior difficulties? What will you do about that?

CHAPTER 4
The Power
of Preparation

CHAPTER 4:
THE POWER OF PREPARATION

The will to win is nothing without the will to prepare to win.
– Vince Lombardi

In the above quote from football coach Vince Lombardi, I want to exchange the word *win* for the word *succeed*. The will to succeed is nothing without the will to prepare to succeed.

Success in All Areas

We can succeed in all areas. "Beloved, I pray that you may prosper in every way and [that your body] may keep well, even as [I know] your soul keeps well and prospers" (3 John 1:2 AMP).

This verse shows that God has made it possible for His children to succeed in life. This means success in every area of our lives is possible – not just success in a career or in a ministry calling, but also in our relationships, our spiritual walk, physical health, and mental health. God wants us to succeed in transforming and renewing our minds, in breaking addictions, in leading a vibrant life, in seeing ourselves as God sees us, and in living significant lives. What is it, then, that prevents most Christians from seeing this promise manifested in their lives? One reason is the lack of preparation. They fail to prepare their souls (mind, will, emotions).

At one time, I believed that accepting Jesus as Lord and Savior guaranteed I would be more than a conquer, an overcomer. As I encountered more and more difficulties, and as I observed other struggling Christians, I realized my choices were involved. The promise of a life of victory in Christ depends on my standing for it, fighting for it, and preparing for it. You can work in a soap factory and still stink; you have to choose to apply the soap.

Await God's Timing

All things begin with a will or strong desire. But no matter how strong the desire, if the timing of what we do is wrong or if the plan is askew, then we will fail. A pie that comes out of the oven before it's cooked, even though it has all the correct ingredients, doesn't taste nearly as good as the one that is fully baked.

When I was fourteen years old, I believed my maturity was sufficient that I could drive one of my mother's work vehicles. I overestimated how long the pie had been in the oven, so to speak. That journey ended when I totaled the car. I was then quite happy to wait for several years to drive again.

It's not too difficult to imagine how different Nehemiah's story would have been if he had chosen to run ahead of God, say, if he had attempted to fix the walls before he had gotten his cupbearer job. He would not have had the protection of the king's soldiers, he would not have been blessed with carts of lumber from the king's forest, and he would not have had special letters of authority from the king.

From the moment Nehemiah arrived in Jerusalem, he encountered strong opposition from the enemies of Judah. But that wasn't his only obstacle. First of all, the sheer magnitude of the job of rebuilding the walls made it seem totally impossible. It lay in a pile of rubble. Another obstacle he faced was a lack of enthusiasm in his own people, those who would benefit the most from a strong, sturdy city wall. How could he deal with these obstacles?

Pray and Fast

Nehemiah would never have made it past these obstacles had he not spent valuable time in preparation. After Nehemiah learned the news about the condition of Jerusalem, he chose to spend four months fasting and praying. Four months! In our present culture of instant this and high-speed that, we often dismiss the need for thorough preparation. If we feel God is calling us to do something, we oftentimes begin without getting clear directions.

I have struggled with this area the most. My nature is to build first and ask questions later. There have been many times when God has revealed something to me and I have ridden off into the sunset to do it, only to realize I'm not sure where I'm going. I've had to learn to take a deep breath and realize the same God who planted the idea is the same God who has a plan to complete it.

Assess the Situation

Once Nehemiah arrived in the city, he invested time not only in prayer but also in carefully assessing the entire situation.

> *I went to Jerusalem, and after staying there three days I set*
> *out during the night with a few others. I had not told anyone what*
> *my God had put in my heart to do for Jerusalem. There were no*
> *mounts with me except the one I was riding on.*
>
> *By night I went out through the Valley Gate toward the Jackal*
> *Well and the Dung Gate, examining the walls of Jerusalem, which*
> *had been broken down, and its gates, which had been destroyed*
> *by fire. Then I moved on toward the Fountain Gate and the King's*
> *Pool, but there was not enough room for my mount to get through;*
> *so I went up the valley by night, examining the wall. Finally, I*
> *turned back and reentered through the Valley Gate. The officials*
> *did not know where I had gone or what I was doing, because as yet*
> *I had said nothing to the Jews or the priests or nobles or officials or*
> *any others who would be doing the work.* (Nehemiah 2:11–16)

In addition to making a careful survey of the situation, Nehemiah took yet another measure of preparation: He kept silent. Verse 16 says, "as yet I said nothing." Oftentimes, we begin talking before God gives us the go-ahead to talk. Talking too soon may bring discouraging words that we're not ready to hear. Talking too soon may take us in a direction that is outside of God's plan.

Part of preparation is listening for God to instruct us when it's time to speak and when it's time to keep silent. "When words are many, sin is not absent, but he who holds his tongue is wise" (Proverbs 10:19). Even evangelist Billy Graham has learned this. He said, "The Christian life is not a constant high. I have my moments of deep discouragement. I have to go to God in prayer with tears in my eyes, and say, 'O God, forgive me,' or 'Help me.'"

Discouraging words came to Nehemiah from his enemies, Sanballat the Hononite, Tobiah the Ammonite official, and Geshem the Arab. Had he not fully prepared his heart and mind regarding God's instructions, Nehemiah would have caved in; he would have given up.

Stop Negative Self-Talk

Discouraging words will not always come from other people. Oftentimes discouraging words come from within our own hearts and minds. We can be our own worst enemies. God speaks a plan or an idea into your heart. Almost immediately the next thought in your mind says, *"There is no way I can do that. I'd love to be a part of something like that, but I'm not qualified. If I do it, it's sure to fail like last time."* No one needs to ridicule your plan because you've already done the job all on your own. A dozen reasons immediately come to mind of why you can't.

The citizens of Jerusalem were looking for excuses. After they learned that Nehemiah had come to rebuild the walls, they began to tell him why they couldn't do the job. "Meanwhile, the people in Judah said, 'The strength of the laborers is giving out, and there is so much rubble that we cannot rebuild the wall'" (Nehemiah 4:10). Essentially, they were saying, "We're too weak and the job's too big."

But Nehemiah had prepared. He had listened to God and he had a plan. Dismissing their excuses, he set about organizing teams of workers. In Nehemiah 4, we see a detailed account of each team (by families), their locations, and their assigned work. Very soon, they were seeing progress; the wall was almost halfway restored.

The most dangerous lies are the lies we believe about ourselves. Our thoughts must line up with what God says about us. We can never accomplish a God-sized plan with a worldly-sized mind.

Our self-talk, the things we tell ourselves, controls the way we feel and act. Nehemiah constantly replaced his thoughts with God's words and, therefore, acted according to God's strength and plan.

Speak the Word of God Aloud

One of the ways I counter the lies and accusations of the enemy is to speak Scripture aloud. There's something about hearing your own voice declaring the truth of God's Word. What follows is a list of some verses I use. Try it yourself in your own quiet time alone with God or the next time you are facing difficulties. Read each verse out loud, and then make a habit of doing this on a regular basis.

Isaiah 41:10 – *Fear not, for I am with you; be not dismayed, for I am your God; I will strengthen you, I will help you, I will uphold you with my righteous right hand.*

Zephaniah 3:17 – *The LORD your God is in your midst, a mighty*

one who will save; he will rejoice over you with gladness; he will
quiet you by his love; he will exult over you with loud singing.

Deuteronomy 31:8 – *It is the LORD who goes before you. He*
will be with you; he will not leave you or forsake you. Do not
fear or be dismayed.

Psalm 9:9 – *The LORD is a stronghold for the oppressed, a*
stronghold in times of trouble. And those who know your name
put their trust in you, for you, O LORD, have not forsaken those
who seek you.

Psalm 23:4 – *Even though I walk through the valley of the*
shadow of death, I will fear no evil, for you are with me; your rod
and your staff, they comfort me.

Psalm 55:22 – *Cast your burden on the LORD, and he will*
sustain you; he will never permit the righteous to be moved.

Matthew 11:28–29 – *Come to me, all who labor and are heavy*
laden, and I will give you rest. Take my yoke upon you, and learn
from me, for I am gentle and lowly in heart, and you will find
rest for your souls.

Threats Bring Fear

The fact that the wall was almost halfway restored should have been
a reason to celebrate, but it only caused the three enemies to intensify their
threats. Now, they threatened physical violence, which produced fear.

"Also our enemies said, 'Before they know it or see us, we will be right
there among them and will kill them and put an end to the work.' Then the
Jews who lived near them came and told us ten times over, 'Wherever you
turn, they will attack us.'" (Nehemiah 4:11–12)

It's interesting to note in the surrounding verses how the Jews in and
around Jerusalem didn't mention the ongoing threat just one time. They
repeated it *ten times.*

Was Nehemiah now exasperated and ready to give up? After all, this is a threat of death. His task has become a matter much larger than building a wall; it has become a matter of survival.

Nehemiah never for a moment was without a plan to move forward. Why? Because he had spent time in preparation. He had the mind of God on this situation, and his confidence in God propelled him forward. As the saying goes, "Don't allow the fear of tomorrow to keep you from exercising your faith today."

Prepare for Battle

In response to this threat, Nehemiah armed the people and organized not just workers but warriors. Nehemiah spoke to the people with words of encouragement: "Don't be afraid of them. Remember the Lord, who is great and awesome, and fight for your families, your sons and your daughters, your wives and your homes" (Nehemiah 4:14 ESV).

From there, Nehemiah communicated his plan:

From that day on, half of my men did the work, while the other half were equipped with spears, shields, bows and armor. The officers posted themselves behind all the people of Judah who were building the wall. Those who carried materials did their work with one hand and held a weapon in the other, and each of the builders wore his sword at his side as he worked. But the man who sounded the trumpet stayed with me. (vv. 16–18)

Part of the plan was to sound the warning at the moment it was time to fight. That's why the man with the trumpet stayed close by.

What happened to the excuses? What happened to the whining and complaining? What happened to the fear and doubt? The man who had prepared in prayer and had spent time in God's presence spoke with such confidence that his words and actions dispelled the fears and doubts.

Keep in mind that Nehemiah had spent most of his adult life as cupbearer to the king. Not a very dangerous position. He probably never had a specific threat on his life before – other than the general risk of the wine being poisoned. Living in the palace near the king was undoubtedly one of the safest places in Shushan.

Now he was facing real life-threatening dangers, and the first person the enemies wanted to kill was the leader. There are consequences when we follow God's leading and direction. We must be ready; we must be prepared. "A righteous man may have many troubles, but the LORD delivers him from them all" (Psalm 34:19).

Take Time to Pray

Our preparation prayer might go something like this: "Lord, I know if I'm going to do what you've called me to do, I'm going to come up against opposition. Show me what I need to be doing now. What can I do today so that I will be ready in the future for what may come against me?"

As you continue praying such a prayer and as you obey God's direction for your preparation, you will not be shocked when you face obstacles. You'll be prepared, and you will be walking in the will of God.

Many Christians I encounter don't want to be bothered with taking time to prepare. For instance, they may be ill and all they want is a quick, instantaneous, miraculous healing.

They think they don't have time to attend a healing service or listen to the audios of a three-week teaching series on healing. They think they don't have time to read books on how to receive healing. They don't have time to look up healing verses in the Bible and meditate on each one. "Lord," they demand, "just give me that instant miracle I need." The truth is, the time to believe for a physical healing is long before you ever need a physical healing. The time to prepare your heart regarding God's truth about healing is when you're feeling great.

You can choose to learn how to believe God for minor pain to be relieved, or a headache to disappear, or a cold to leave your body. Begin with small victories, which build your faith in these areas. Then you are prepared to say, "God, I know you answered prayer in this small area before, and now I have faith that you can answer prayer in this big area over here." This is how we choose to prepare.

Learning how to renew our minds according to God's promises is preparation. Learning how to pray Scripture verses so that our prayers are in accordance with His will is preparation. Learning how to wait on God and listen for His voice and direction is preparation.

When the enemy comes and puts thoughts in your head that you're a loser, a failure, you'll never amount to anything, or you can never succeed, then you'll instantly have the answer. "I'm a child of the King of kings; I am more than a conqueror; I am fearfully and wonderfully made; The Lord upholds me with His righteous right hand; I have been created to do good works."

If you are in the middle of the battle without preparation, then pray for wisdom. Seek God earnestly for His plan, and He will see you through. In Mark 9:24, we find a father in the same situation, who simply said, "Lord, help my unbelief."

David's Years of Preparation

King David learned this lesson of preparation and progression as a young shepherd boy out in the fields caring for his father's flocks. We sometimes think that David's preparation to kill the giant was going to the brook to find five stones. But his preparation time began long before that moment.

David's attitude was one of love and adoration for his God. Imagine how different his life would have been if he'd said, "One of these days when I don't have to be a shepherd boy, I'm going to write songs to God. I'm going to sing praises and spend time with God. I'll do all that just as soon as I can get out of this dumb sheep job."

Instead, he spent his days singing praises, worshipping, writing poetry, and trusting God. Then what happened? A dangerous lion came along and attacked the sheep. That had to have been a terrifying experience.

Again, let's imagine if David had said, "So much for this praise and worship thing, God. I spent time in praise and worship and You sent a wild animal that nearly killed me. Couldn't You have kept the lion away? As if that wasn't enough, I had to face a bear. What's going on here? Where's Your protection, God? I'm just not into this anymore. It must not work. I think I'll go do my own thing."

Could this be said about many of us? When the going gets tough, we step back and say, "This just isn't working. I'm out of here."

In the Bible, we have the advantage of seeing the full picture of David's life. We realize God was preparing him with these wild animals so that one day when he faced the giant, he had total faith that his God would deliver him. It was because of preparation time, and because of a progression of small victories to larger victories that David was ready to face a giant.

How to Prepare

How do you prepare? Time in prayer. Time reading God's Word. Time meditating on God's Word, letting the Word take root in your heart, and praising God for all He has already done. Let the Word transform your mind. Spend time alone with God, listening for His voice.

Don't fall into the trap of thinking that listening to Christian teaching and reading Christian books is all that's needed. I can read a hundred books about prayer and know exactly how to pray, but if I don't ever actually spend time in prayer, that reading has no value. The same can be said about knowing the Bible. As a Christian, you may have extensive knowledge of the Bible, but if you never put that knowledge into action, then it will bring little value to your life. When we act on our knowledge, transformation takes place.

Prepare by asking God to guide you. No matter what you do, ask God to show you the way. As you enter into a conversation with someone or before you go to a meeting with a group of people, ask for His guidance and His wisdom.

When you get an idea about something, have the courage to pray: "Lord, here's what I think I want, but I'm bringing this before You. I want to know if this is Your best plan for my life. I don't want anything that's not Your will."

Once you begin to enter into preparation in that way, you'll miss out on a great deal of frustration. The Lord may say, "This is not the right time just now," or He may reveal to you an even better plan.

Remember 3 John 1:2 tells us the secret to prosper in every area of our lives is to keep our souls prospering. That will only happen if we're willing to take the time in preparation. We can see from the life of Nehemiah that due to his diligence in being prepared, he was successful in all aspects of his life. He helped transform the course of an entire nation.

Reflection Questions

1. Describe a time when you failed to prepare. What was the result?
2. In what ways are you preparing today for where God may lead you tomorrow?

CHAPTER 5

Needing the Anointing

CHAPTER 5:
NEEDING THE ANOINTING

The highest form of worship is the worship of unselfish Christian service. The greatest form of praise is the sound of consecrated feet seeking out the lost and helpless.
— Billy Graham

Have you ever wondered why the Jerusalem city walls had remained a pile of rubble for so many years before Nehemiah's time? One hundred years had passed since the city had been ransacked and the Israelites had been taken captive to Babylon. Of the remnant that stayed behind, was there no one who thought it would be a good idea to rebuild the walls? Evidently not. Why not?

First, I'm sure the undertaking seemed too big. It appeared to be an impossible task. Second, the people were divided. No one was in agreement as to how this herculean job could be completed. What was missing?

An Anointed Leader

An anointed leader was missing, one who was called and anointed by God. Nehemiah was that leader. Nehemiah spent four months in prayer and fasting about the problem. This is where the anointing comes from; it is birthed in prayer.

In our church world, the word *anointing* is often bandied about with no real thought of what it means. In a healing service, we often pray for people and anoint them with oil according to James 5:14: "Is any sick among you? Let them call for the elders of the church and let them pray over them anointing them with oil in the name of the Lord."

What Anointing Is and Is Not

While using oil in prayer for healing is an important anointing, it's not the one I'm talking about here. I'm referring to the anointing described in 1 John 2:27: "As for you, the anointing you received from Him remains in you, and you do not need anyone to teach you. But as His anointing teaches you about all things and as that anointing is real, not counterfeit – just as it has taught you, remain in Him."

This anointing is not something we can go to a church service and receive. It *could* be imparted in a corporate worship time, but more often it is cultivated and nurtured over years of consistent discipline in prayer. Every Christian can operate in the anointing of God, just as Jesus did.

Luke 4:18–19 tells us what Jesus said about His own anointing: "The Spirit of the Lord is upon me, because He hath anointed me to preach the gospel to the poor; He hath sent me to heal the brokenhearted, to preach deliverance to the captives, and recovering of sight to the blind, to set at liberty them that are bruised, to preach the acceptable year of the Lord."

From these verses we can see what God's anointing enables us to do. If we attempt to witness to people outside of God's anointing, it's like the sound of fingernails on a chalkboard. If you try to help people get free from depression, healed of a broken heart, or free from disillusionment, but don't have God's anointing, nothing will result.

When we try to do things in our own strength, what happens? We get disappointed because nothing happens. If we are going to go against the odds and succeed, then it's going to take God's anointing. Oftentimes when we face big problems we attempt to tackle them in our own strength, using our own plans and ideas. Then we end up making the problem worse. But if we take the time to pray, seek God's face, and listen for His answer, then it's amazing how He makes a way where there seemed to be no way before.

God Will Make a Way

When I was a boy, I remember a song we sang in our church. The lyrics went like this:

God will make a way
Where there seems to be no way
He works in ways we cannot see
He will make a way for me
He will be my guide
Hold me closely to His side
With love and strength
For each new day
He will make a way
He will make a way

– Don Moen

This wasn't just a song we sang; those words ministered faith to me and built hope in my heart. When I was a preschooler living in South Africa, my father decided he no longer wanted me and my family around. My mother, my brother Clint, and I were put out on the street. We had no home. In my natural world, there seemed to be no way.

We three shared one bed at my uncle's house. My mother worked whatever jobs she could find. Even under those circumstances we had absolute faith that God would make a way for us. Thus began a life of believing God for daily provisions. It was a time of preparation for me. In spite of this seeming lack and deprivation, my brother and I felt we were the luckiest kids on earth. Not a day went by that God didn't supply something in a miraculous way, whether it was a roof over our heads, gas for the car, or groceries on the table.

We had a prayer list longer than the Mississippi River, but we didn't just pray for our needs. Each night we prayed for other people we knew who needed breakthroughs in their lives.

Through those lean years, God made a way for us time and time again. I could write an entire book just relating all the miracles due solely to God's power and His anointing. Miracles cannot happen in our own power any more than we can operate an electric lawn mower without plugging it in. God's anointing is the power source!

When the children of Israel were in the wilderness and God instructed them to build the tabernacle, the craftsmen were anointed of God to do the work. (See Exodus 35 and 36.) The anointing of God is not only for spiritual matters but for practical tasks as well. God wants to show the carpenter, the business owner, the attorney, the parent, or whomever how to do the work better. The anointing of God covers all areas of our lives. It's the anointing that sets Christians apart from the world. Likewise, it is the absence of the anointing that makes us look and act like the rest of the world.

When we operate under the anointing of God, He goes before us and prepares the way. If you're facing a mountain of obstacles, God will get you through or over or around that mountain. In your own strength you'll only struggle, and it could cost years of frustrated effort and wasted energy.

Examples of God's Anointing

Most of us have read the story of David killing Goliath so often we tend to trivialize what happened in this battle. In actuality, it was totally impossible for the boy David to kill that giant with one small stone. But with God's anointing on his life, it became possible. We read stories all through the Bible of individuals who accomplished amazing feats because they operated under the anointing of God.

In 2 Chronicles 20 we see how Jehoshaphat defeated three different armies at once and never even had to fight a battle. Through prayer and fasting and listening to God, King Jehoshaphat knew what to do. God gave him a wild and crazy plan. Jehoshaphat was instructed to appoint men to sing to the Lord and to praise Him. Not only that, but these singers were to march ahead of the army!

God's anointing was in the plan. As they sang, God caused the armies who were coming toward them to turn and fight and kill one another. The Israelites never had to lift a finger against their enemies. Among the slain, Jehoshaphat's army found a great amount of equipment and clothing and other articles of value. The Bible says, "There was so much plunder that it took three days to collect it" (2 Chronicles 20:25). This is what happens when we do things God's way.

There's another account in God's Word that shows what happens when God's leading and guiding is and is not taken into consideration. In Joshua 6, we see how the children of Israel entered into the Promised Land and defeated the fortified city of Jericho by listening to and obeying God. They marched around the city once a day for six days. On the seventh day, they marched around the walled city seven times. On the seventh time around, they sounded the trumpets and sent up a loud shout. When they did, the walls fell and they overtook the city.

Going in Our Own Strength

The next city on their list was the small village of Ai. Still rejoicing from their victory over Jericho, the Israelites chose not to pray, not to ask God for guidance. They did not seek God's anointing. In fact, after spying out the place, they decided only a small army was needed to wipe out the city.

When they returned to Joshua, they said, "Not all the army will have to go up against Ai. Send two or three thousand men to take it and do not weary the whole army, for only a few people live there." So about three thousand went up; but they were routed by the men of Ai, who killed about thirty-six of them. They chased the Israelites from the city gate as far as the stone quarries and struck them down on the slopes. At this the hearts of the people melted in fear and became like water. (Joshua 7:3–5)

Had Joshua taken the time to pray and seek God's face, thirty-six men would not have lost their lives. He would have known that one of his soldiers had sinned by stealing forbidden plunder from the city of Jericho. The protection of God had been lifted, but no one knew it.

How often do we get overconfident in our own abilities? "I've got this one, Lord. You can take the day off." When we take on that attitude, we're headed for defeat. It's important to know and understand that there's really no time in our lives, no situation, when we do not need God's anointing. Jesus makes this point clear in John 15:4–5: "I am the vine; you are the branches. If you remain in me and I in you, you will bear much fruit; apart from me you can do nothing."

Notice Jesus didn't say "apart from me you can do a few things." He was specific that apart from Him we can do absolutely nothing. So why try?

My Personal Lesson

I learned this lesson the hard way. God had been blessing my church's Sunday evening service. After years of seeing only a handful of people attend, the church was starting to experience growth. More people began to attend and many took the time to comment on the quality of the preaching.

I received a text message one day letting me know that an individual, who was considered important in certain Christian circles, would be attending the next Sunday. Because the services had been going so well and because I felt my preaching was improving, I decided to preach my best sermon ever. (Notice I said that I decided.) I wanted to show this special guest just how anointed I really was.

Any guesses as to how that service turned out? Half way through, I just wanted to turn off the lights and go home. I had prepared so hard to make sure the sermon was impressive, and in doing so I traded God's transforming power for my own wisdom and ability. It was awful, to say the least, and I learned a hard lesson. I repented and assured God I would never do that again. It was never more true to me that outside of God and

His anointing, I have absolutely nothing to offer.

All through the book of Nehemiah, we see a man who is confident in every area and in meeting every obstacle in his path. As we take a closer look, we see that he did none of it in his own power. At no time did he allow pride to rule nor did he assume he could handle it on his own. He totally leaned on the Lord and rested in the confidence that God's anointing would succeed against the odds.

In the same way, each one of us needs God's anointing.

Trying to Produce Fruit

In John 15:5, Jesus tells us we "will bear much fruit." The problem comes when we misunderstand the term bear. In this particular verse, bear does not mean produce; it means to carry. (The Greek word is phero, meaning to carry.)

If you studied biology in school, you learned that the branch does not produce the fruit; it merely holds the fruit. It's the vine that produces the fruit. In my life, I have often tried to produce God's fruit, such as love, joy, peace, and so on. I'm sure you can relate. You want to be more patient with family members or coworkers, so you make the decision to *be more patient.* Does it work? Your human effort will carry you for a while, but eventually it's doomed to fail.

I have tried in my own strength to produce anointed, life-changing preaching, but that's not my job. My job is to carry and present what God is doing on the inside of me. It's His job to do the producing; it is my job to do the desiring. I can no more produce fruits and gifts of the Spirit than I can lay an egg, but that doesn't stop me from eagerly seeking them in prayer and expecting God to do His part. (See 1 Corinthians 12:31; 14:1) The greatest sermons I have ever preached were always the ones where I did far more praying and far less writing. I let God do it.

George Mueller

In the 1800s, a man named George Mueller became the pastor of a small church in England. The church planned to pay him a good salary from the money it received from renting pews. In those days rich church members sat at the front of the church and paid a substantial sum to rent the best pews. The poorer members had to sit in the "cheap" seats at the back.

George told the church leaders that this practice had to stop if they wanted him to be their pastor. Even so, he refused their salary offer, choosing rather to trust God to meet his needs. And God did just that. George and his family never missed a meal and were always able to pay their rent. Soon, however, George began to sense that God had something else for him to do.

Each day as George was out walking, he saw orphans living on the streets or in state-run poorhouses where they were treated inhumanely. George felt God calling him to open an orphanage to take care of these children.

George began to pray, asking God to provide a building, people to oversee the work, furniture, and money for food and clothing. God answered his prayers. As the work grew, the needs of the orphanage were met on a daily basis without George announcing to anyone about his needs. He just prayed and waited on God.

Through the years, more than 10,000 children lived in the orphanage. When each child became old enough to live on his own, George would put a Bible in his right hand and a coin in his left. He explained to the young person that if he held onto what was in his right hand, God would always make sure there was something in his left. George then prayed and sent him on his way.

When George Muller started the orphanage, he had only the equivalent of fifty cents in his pocket, but he never had a shortage of prayer. God's anointing did what no human effort ever could.

Heidi Baker

Heidi Baker, a missionary to Mozambique, had spent years of her life pouring out everything she had but had seen few results. She was desperately trying to help the broken, lost, and orphaned children of that country. She literally worked herself into an emotional and physical collapse and still had little to show for her efforts.

She returned to her home in Canada physically sick, defeated, and exhausted. One night during a church service she learned the answer to her dilemma. The missing element had been God's anointing, God's ability. She realized she had been trying to do the work in her own power.

Armed with this fresh new truth in her heart, she returned to Mozambique.

Within a few short years, she had planted more than 5,000 churches!

I have visited her work there and have seen the orphanages myself. They are remarkable. They rescue children who have been raped, forced to murder, and undergone the worst things imaginable, Yet, when you meet the children, all you see is the transforming power of God. How many years of counseling would it take to achieve these kinds of emotional healing? God's anointing can do in five minutes what we couldn't do in years of our own efforts.

Reflection Questions

1. Have you ever experienced working for or with an anointed leader? What was it like?
2. Recall a time when you did something in your own power without God's anointing. What happened?
3. How are you approaching the challenges in your life now? In your own power or with God's anointing?
4. Are you asking God to empower you? If not, why not?

CHAPTER 6
Learning Our Role

CHAPTER 6: LEARNING OUR ROLE

Don't wait for extraordinary circumstance to do good;
start with the ordinary situations.
                                                    – Charles Richter

When Nehemiah arrived on the Jerusalem scene, he organized the people so that each family and each person knew his or her job in the building process. In Nehemiah 3, we see a list of every family and their particular assignment. Everyone set about doing his or her part in the restoration of the wall.

In Western culture, we don't typically have large families or live in large family clans. We often don't even know our extended relatives. That means this idea from Nehemiah does not apply to us. Right? Wrong.

The Body of Christ

Believers in Christ are part of a large family, worldwide, in fact. In 1 Corinthians 12:15–27, Paul explains that we are the body of Christ and that each and every member has a role to play.

Now if the foot should say, "Because I am not a hand, I do not belong to the body," it would not for that reason stop being part of the body. And if the ear should say, "Because I am not an eye, I do not belong to the body," it would not for that reason stop being part of the body. If the whole body were an eye, where would the sense of hearing be? If the whole body were an ear, where would the sense of smell be? But in fact God has placed the parts in the body, every one of them, just as he wanted them to be. If they were all one part, where would the body be? As it is, there are many parts, but one body.

The eye cannot say to the hand, "I don't need you!" And the head cannot say to the feet, "I don't need you!" On the contrary, those parts of the body that seem to be weaker are indispensable, and the parts that we think are less honorable we treat with special honor. And the parts that are unpresentable are treated with special modesty, while our presentable parts need no special treatment. But God has put the body together, giving greater honor to the parts that lacked it, so that there should be no

*division in the body, but that its parts should have equal concern
for each other. If one part suffers, every part suffers with it; if one
part is honored, every part rejoices with it.*

*Now you are the body of Christ, and each one of you is a
part of it.*

Paul makes it clear that no Christian has a right to say he or she is not
needed or that he or she has nothing to offer.

Throughout the history of the church, huge revivals have literally swept
through a country. While it may have appeared that one single evangelist
headed up a revival, careful examination proves all revivals started with
a group of people dedicated to prayer and intercession. Where did such
intercessors come from? They were individuals who never questioned
whether or not they had something to offer. They gave of their time, their
effort, their concern, and their desire to see people saved for all eternity.

We learn more about doing our part in James 2:14–18:

*What good is it, my brothers and sisters, if someone claims to
have faith but has no deeds? Can such faith save them? Suppose
a brother or a sister is without clothes and daily food. If one of
you says to them, "Go in peace; keep warm and well fed," but does
nothing about their physical needs, what good is it? In the same
way, faith by itself, if it is not accompanied by action, is dead. But
someone will say, "You have faith; I have deeds." Show me your
faith without deeds, and I will show you my faith by my deeds.*

Once we pray, once we stand by faith that God will answer our prayers,
then it's time to act in accordance with our prayers.

The Seed Principle

What is our part? That question can be answered easily when you
understand that everything in the kingdom of God operates on the seed
principle. The seed principle has been with us since the Garden of Eden.
"Then God said, 'I give you every seed-bearing plant on the face of the
whole earth and every tree that has fruit with seed in it. They will be yours
for food'" (Genesis 1:29).

Why did God create the seed principle? So that we could partner with God in all that He is doing. Planting seeds requires something from each of us. But even in the process of planting seeds, we must be clear on what is our part and what is God's part. We can plant, but we cannot create the miracle of germination. We can water, but we cannot create the miracle of life and growth. As we enter into the planting partnership, we must try not to do God's part.

A Seed of Oil

An amazing story in the Old Testament clearly demonstrates the seed principle. A widow with two sons has just been threatened by her creditors that they are coming to take her sons. The story opens in 2 Kings 4 as this widow is pleading with the prophet Elisha to help her.

Many of us know what it's like to get behind on our bills. Some of us may even know how the finances are stretched after a spouse (possibly the breadwinner of the family) has died. As frightening as that may be, however, we have not experienced a creditor threatening to take our children and make them slaves. This widow was facing a terrifying situation.

Elisha let her know that she had a part to play in her own solution. He asked her what she had in her house. Why would he ask such a question? She is obviously poor, but Elisha knows she must have a seed that can be planted for her miracle to come forth.

At first, she answers, "Your servant has nothing at all." This is so true for many of us. We think we have no talent, no abilities, nothing to offer to the kingdom. We see ourselves as lacking, coming up empty.

After a moment, the widow adds, "except a small jar of olive oil."

Bingo! That's what Elisha was waiting for. He was waiting for her to discover what she had to offer the Lord. Now, it's time to set things in motion for the miracle to happen.

> Elisha said, "Go around and ask all your neighbors for empty jars. Don't ask for just a few. Then go inside and shut the door behind you and your sons. Pour oil into all the jars, and as each is filled, put it to one side."
>
> She left him and shut the door behind her and her sons. They brought the jars to her and she kept pouring. When all the jars were full, she said to her son, "Bring me another one." But he replied, "There is not a jar left." Then the oil stopped flowing. (2 Kings 4:3–6)

The Courage to Obey

Beyond realizing that she had some oil, the widow had to take another step. She had to have the courage to go to her neighbors and borrow empty jars. The whole neighborhood knew she was in debt. What did they think when she came asking to borrow jars? She could have stopped at Elisha's request, but she did not. At this point, what did she have to lose?

She and her sons borrowed jars, went inside the house, closed the door, and began to pour. The oil flowed until every jar was filled to the brim. All because she was willing to give the last bit of her oil – all she had in her possession at that moment. She did her part. After she did, God stepped in and did His part.

This widow who had nothing was in the olive oil business! "She went and told the man of God, and he said, 'Go, sell the oil and pay your debts. You and your sons can live on what is left'" (2 Kings 4:7).

I find it amazing that God leaves it up to us how much we want to experience. The amount of oil the widow had was in direct proportion to the amount of her faith and courage and hard work in asking her neighbors for jars. If the widow had little faith and much timidity, she would have stopped asking after she got a few jars and would have had much less oil.

In Matthew 9:29, Jesus touched the eyes of two blind men and said, "According to your faith will it be done to you." If they believed they would gain their sight, then they did. The miracle was according to the measure of *their* faith.

We see this principal played out again and again. A woman is healed because she believed that touching Jesus' robe would produce healing. A centurion believed that it was enough if Jesus just spoke the word and his child would be healed. Do you expect God to show up by the measure of faith you have? Or do you limit what He can do through you? What would have happened if the widow had another thirty jars? There would have been another thirty jars of worth of oil available.

How much of God do you want?

Giving Our Seed

It's so easy for us to think that others have all the gifts and talents. All God is looking for from you is your small seed. I'm convinced that if you have a gift of baking gingerbread men and you give that talent to the Lord, He will use it mightily for the kingdom. All of a sudden, your gingerbread men will take on eternal significance for God's kingdom purposes although you may never see all the results in this life.

When you say to God, "This is all I have, but I give it to you," then God says, "Great. That's all I want." There's no excuse for any of us not to succeed against the odds, because God is on our side. He will take whatever we offer to Him and use it for His glory.

If God is not showing up in your life to manifest miracles, then it may be because there's no room for Him. We become satisfied with status quo. We make no new space for Him to do a miracle in our lives.

A Better Covenant

As amazing as this oil-business miracle was, Christians today are in a better covenant. As Hebrews 7:22 says, "Because of this oath, Jesus has become the guarantor of a better covenant."

A *better covenant* means that whatever problems we are facing, God is more than enough. We no longer have to go through a human priest to gain access to God and we don't have to bring an animal to sacrifice. "But in fact the ministry Jesus has received is as superior to [the Israelites] as the covenant of which he is mediator is superior to the old one, since the new covenant is established on better promises" (Hebrews 8:6).

We can go to God directly through prayer. When we give Him access into our problem, it doesn't matter what odds we're facing, God is facing them as well. He goes before us.

The Tithe Seed

Have you ever wondered why God instituted the tithe? God doesn't have a mortgage, does He? He didn't buy heaven from someone and now needs our help to pay off the debt. We're not helping Him pay the utility bills. Or His phone bill. He doesn't need our money.

God instituted the tithe to allow you and me to plant a seed into the kingdom. Planting the seed is our part. Then God says, "Thank you for that seed. Now let Me give you a harvest." The monetary seed that we plant gives God access into our finances.

The Time Seed

Do you know why it's important to pray and spend time with God each morning? It becomes our seed which then gives God access to come into our day and make a difference. When you pray, you are literally injecting God into your situation.

Oftentimes we spend more time worrying than we spend praying. Worry is ridiculous; yet, we all do it because we don't take God at His word. I've never heard of anyone who reported great accomplishments due to spending an entire night in worry. On the other hand, I've heard many testimonies of miraculous deeds done as a result of spending an entire night in prayer. Our time in prayer is one seed we sow that allows God to work in our lives.

In Matthew 6:25–34, Jesus commands us not to worry. Why? Because worry produces fear, and fear causes paralysis or drawing back from where we are heading. Worry stops fruit from being produced in our lives (Mark 4:19). Worry shows lack of faith in God.

When we worry and try to solve our problems in our own energy, the problems worsen. We're in too much of a hurry to stop and pray. Our to-do list is too full. Our desk at work is filled with stacks of too-much-to-do. We think God will understand, but my boss will not. The truth is, the more time we give to God, the less time we have to spend on our problems.

This little poem by Grace L. Naessens says it all:
I got up early one morning and rushed right into the day!
I had so much to accomplish that I didn't have time to pray.
Problems just tumbled about me, and heavier came each task.
"Why doesn't God help me?" I wondered.
He answered, "You didn't ask!"
I tried to come into God's presence; I used all my keys at the lock.
God gently and lovingly chided, "Why, child, you didn't knock!"
I wanted to see joy and beauty, but the day toiled on, gray and bleak.
I wondered why God didn't show me.
He said, "But you didn't seek."
I woke up early this morning, and paused before entering the day.
I had so much to accomplish that I had to take time to pray!

Restoring God's Kingdom

All through Nehemiah 3, we see that each family group knew their part in the restoration of the walls, gates, and doors. No one slacked off; no one complained. Every person set his or her hand to the task.

Are we doing our part to restore that which God has given us to restore? He has given us the mandate and the ability to restore the kingdom of God. Are we doing our part? It's not all about preaching. It's not all about worship. It's about praying. It's about encouragement. It's about receiving a word from God for someone. It's about praying for the sick. It's about giving somebody a Scripture verse at the right time. It's about praying over your workplace. It's about changing people's circumstances through the power of God.

How does your section of the wall look today? Is your family a solid gate, or are there holes where the enemy can break through? Is your prayer life a solid gate, or does your area give the enemy easy access? What about your finances? Or your thoughts? The list can go on and on. Check to see that the place where you are building (doing your part) is strong and secure.

What is your seed? Ask God what He has designed for you to do. Your seed is your seed. It may not look like your spouse's seed or your friend's seed or your pastor's seed. Every person in God's kingdom has seed to sow and likewise has great harvests to reap, but a harvest can never grow if the seed is never planted.

International Ministry

A few weeks after I was kicked out of my church, I was sitting at home, feeling disillusioned and confused. My mother said, "Son, what's in your hand?" This is the same question God asked Moses in Exodus 4:2. My mother was showing me the seed I had in my life that I must plant in order for God to bring a harvest. I had a degree in software engineering in my hand, and I had a video camera.

With these, I launched PhillipsPower.com and began uploading messages that I recorded while sitting at the coffee table. I never knew if anyone would watch these videos, but it was in my hand and so I decided to use it. During one of the times when I felt the most dejected, I recorded a video on salvation where I led the viewer through the Scriptures and the steps to accept Jesus Christ as Savior.

One day I received an email from a ministry in India. The email said that they had found my website and wanted me to come preach in the south of India. I thought it was a spam email, because who was I to go preach? A nobody who didn't even have a church. But there was something about that email. I couldn't let it go.

Eventually, my mom and I agreed together that we would pursue it. Then came the email asking for money so they could rent venues. There it was; I had been waiting for that part. I still thought it might be a trick. After praying, we agreed to send the money. It was money I had to borrow, because I was still unemployed in spite of multiple efforts otherwise.

We arrived in India at a little village airport. We looked around for a sign with our names, but there was nothing. My heart dropped. It must have been a scam, and I was disappointed because I so wanted to be used by God.

My mom decided that we had come too far not to have some fun, and so we decided to take a taxi somewhere. We climbed into the taxi. I explained our destination, and the taxi driver nodded. The destination was at least real. Two hours later we pulled into the town, and to our amazement big posters hung on the walls of the town: "Pastor Brent and Maureen Phillips from USA." Their request had been real; it was exactly what they had said it would be!

For the next week, we ministered all over the south of India, seeing God transform lives and save people. It was, to this day, one of my most life-changing experiences.

Three weeks following our return home, a tsunami hit that area of India, killing thousands of people. As I heard the news, I wept thinking of all those people we'd come to know. Then God showed me it was not a time of mourning but a time of rejoicing, because those who were lost had been found!

This verse came to mind: "Now to Him who is able to do immeasurably more than all we ask or imagine, according to His power that is at work within us" (Ephesians 3:20).

Reflection Questions

1. Until now, have you typically told God you have nothing to offer or that you are willing to use what you have?
2. What seed(s) do you have in your life right now? If you have trouble knowing, ask God to show you the seed you have.
3. What is God asking you to do with your seed to bring about an abundant harvest?
4. How much faith do you have in believing God can use your seed to create a miracle?

CHAPTER 7

Co-Laboring with Christ

CHAPTER 7: CO-LABORING WITH CHRIST

When in doubt, don't.
— Benjamin Franklin

Nehemiah became a history maker in part because he knew, beyond a doubt, that he and God were working together.

Have you ever stepped out to take action, and once the obstacles rose up, once the problems appeared, you stepped back and wondered, *Where is God in all of this?*

No Misgivings

We see no indication that Nehemiah ever struggled with misgivings.

Therefore, I stationed some of the people behind the lowest points of the wall at the exposed places, posting them by families, with their swords, spears and bows. After I looked things over, I stood up and said to the nobles, the officials and the rest of the people, "Don't be afraid of [the enemies]. Remember the Lord, who is great and awesome, and fight for your families, your sons and your daughters, your wives and your homes." (Nehemiah 4:13–14)

When the circumstances turned violent and dangerous, notice how Nehemiah encouraged the workers, reminding them that God was *working with* them. "Remember the Lord," he tells them.

In the next verse Nehemiah attributes their victory to God. "When our enemies heard that we were aware of their plot and that God had frustrated it, we all returned to the wall, each to our own work" (v. 15).

When we choose to co-labor with the Lord, He will be there with us in the midst of the obstacles and in the victories.

The Team of Ezra and Nehemiah

Prior to Nehemiah's presence in Jerusalem, the prophet Ezra had made the journey with a number of those who had been in exile. In the Hebrew

Bible, the two books of Ezra and Nehemiah are one book. Ezra came to the city to restore worship. He brought with him many of the artifacts used in temple worship that had been carried away by King Nebuchadnezzar of Babylon. Nebuchadnezzar was responsible for the destruction of the city of Jerusalem, especially the destruction of the glorious temple that had been built by Solomon. With Ezra's return, a new temple had been built but the city walls lay in ruin.

Nehemiah became known as the one responsible for the rebuilding of the wall. He helped to reestablish, according to God's purpose and plan, the glorious city of Jerusalem. As a co-laborer with God, Nehemiah had the privilege of listening to God. He stepped forward, joined God's work, and accomplished something that was recorded in the annals of history not only in the Bible but in history books.

Created for Good Works

A study of Nehemiah demonstrates what co-laboring with God is all about. After Jesus fills our hearts, He doesn't expect us to live a comfortable, mundane life. All of His vast treasure of power and promises belongs to us. He expects us to be history makers like Nehemiah.

Those of us who are redeemed by the blood of Jesus are capable of changing the course of history. Ephesians 2:10 tells us that we were created for good works. God has good works that He planned for us to do. These good works have the potential to change history. The word good in the Greek is agathos, which is the same word used in Genesis when God looked at creation and saw that it was good! We are not talking about "nice"; we are talking about phenomenal, life-changing works that God has prepared for us to do.

Are we living with that kind of passion and expectancy? In John 10:10, Jesus promises that our lives can be abundant. That abundant life comes when we co-labor with Jesus in all facets of our lives.

In this day and age, our churches are filled with people who claim the name of Jesus. They worship His name, but living the Christian life seems to be too hard for them. Instead, we should think of life as a vibrant, exciting battle we are winning for all eternity. We're working for *eternity*. This means the love and compassion of Christ overwhelms our hearts; rivers of living water stream out from us, bringing life and transformation to all those around us. When you influence others for good, you are changing history – their history.

You can live a life of significance the moment you partner with God. All through the Bible we see instance after instance where God delights to lay hold of a seemingly insignificant person and make of that person a history changer.

He wants to do the same thing for each one of us. But first we must learn what it means to co-labor with God. It's not simply doing good works; it's not just stepping out and serving; it's not just meeting needs that we see around us. Co-laboring with God can and does *include* those actions, but more importantly it's about getting in tune with the Father's heart. Then God, in His unique way and in His perfect time, will lay something on your heart and your heart will burn. You will feel *compelled* to do something. You will be driven by the power of the Holy Spirit.

Spirit Inspired

One of the components of co-laboring with Jesus is that the job must be Spirit-inspired. Much of what we see happening in our churches can be accomplished completely by human endeavors. This is a far cry from what is recorded in the book of Acts. In this action-filled book, we read about Spirit-inspired miracles on nearly every page.

Please don't misunderstand. I'm not referring to contrived sensationalism just to get attention. I'm talking about seeking God, hungering for His manifested presence and waiting on Him until we hear His voice.

This is exactly what Nehemiah did. Once he heard about the plight of his people and the city of God, Jerusalem, he became broken. He wept and grieved. When was the last time that we were so moved that we wept and grieved before God? We are Christians who, for the most part, have lost the ability to grieve over the injustices and the tragedies all around us. (See 2 Chronicles 7:14.)

Part of the reason we don't grieve is due to our being deluged with images on TV, computers, and mobile devices. We see people dying of hunger, thousands of people homeless due to earthquakes, wars, and bombings. So what happens? We become desensitized. Our hearts are no longer moved. We stop asking ourselves, "Where's my heart in all of this?"

When we hear of a suicide in our community, is our heart broken? When we hear of families breaking up, are we in intercession for them? We know the thief comes to kill, steal, and destroy (John 10:10), so it's our place and position to stand in the gap for a lost and dying world.

Why are our hearts not heavy, realizing that people all around us have no sense of fulfillment in life? They have so many material goods, but they have no peace in their hearts. That fact should drive us to our knees. We should fast and pray. We should get closely connected with the heart of our Lord Jesus, who wept over humanity. It's time to get connected with the Father's heart, so we can hear His wooing, His specific commission, His unique calling, and become Spirit-inspired.

In the last chapter, we saw that Nehemiah rode secretly through the rubble on horseback as he surveyed the damage. In Nehemiah 2:12, he said that he had told no one "what God had put in my heart to do at Jerusalem." This statement is positive proof that he was confident that he was a co-laborer with God in all that he was doing. He knew that in and of himself, he could never have come up with such an amazing plan. We often get this turned around. We try to put our own desire into God's heart. We try to talk Him into taking up our plans and purposes.

Beyond Our Talents

Another aspect of co-laboring with God is that He will take us far beyond what our talents are seemingly capable of. Remember that Nehemiah presumably knew little or nothing about being a leader, building a wall, or fighting a war. This didn't faze God; He chose Nehemiah for the job anyway.

If it were up to me to choose someone to build a massive wall around an entire city, I would probably seek out someone who had at least some wall-building experience. But it was Nehemiah who wept, grieved, and poured his heart out to God. It was Nehemiah who connected with the heart of his Father God. It was Nehemiah that God called, and Nehemiah that God used.

"For the eyes of the LORD run to and fro throughout the whole earth, to show himself strong in the behalf of them whose heart is perfect toward him" (2 Chronicles 16:9). This verse tells us that God is searching out those whose hearts are turned toward Him. It doesn't say He's searching for the most talented, the best looking, or the most silver-tongued orator. It's a heart matter.

There's no limit to what you can do in this world. Absolutely no limit. The only factor for all of us is if we are obedient to step into that place, allow God to move in our hearts, and then wait for His commission. When we do, He will co-labor with us.

Direct Spiritual Warfare

When we move into position to co-labor with Christ, we can be assured there will be spiritual warfare. Jesus said, "Remember the word that I said unto you, 'The servant is not greater than his lord.' If they have persecuted me, they will also persecute you" (John 15:20). Paul echoes this idea in 2 Timothy 3:12: "In fact, everyone who wants to live a godly life in Christ Jesus will be persecuted."

Nehemiah certainly experienced persecution, but he assured the people, "Our God will fight for us." He was confident that he was teamed up with the God of the universe and that God would fight the battles for them. Each and every time, God came through and the wall was completed.

The Spiritual Battle

Today, we don't do battle as they did in the Old Testament. Ours is a spiritual battle. Paul reminds us in Ephesians 6:12 that our struggle is not against flesh and blood, but against the rulers, against the authorities, against the powers of this dark world, and against the spiritual forces of evil in the heavenly realms. When you come against the forces of darkness, you cannot effectually do battle in your own strength. You can do that only by co-laboring with God.

In the Western church today, we have become too comfortable. We've lost the sense of urgency to win the lost and save them from an eternity away from God.

Nehemiah's purpose in rebuilding the wall was to provide physical safety, saving the citizens of the city from enemy attacks and physical death. Our battle is different, but it requires the same passion. We are in a battle to push back the powers of darkness and wage war for souls, to plunder hell and populate heaven.

In Matthew 17, we find an account of Jesus' disciples attempting unsuccessfully to heal a demon-possessed boy. When Jesus appeared on the scene, the demon left at Jesus' word. Later, the disciples asked why they were unable to drive out the demon. (Prior to this, these disciples had been instrumental in many healing miracles.) Jesus explained that there are some instances where only *prayer and fasting* will do the job.

It's important to notice that Jesus did not say that they might win a few and lose a few. He did not say that sometimes God puts a disease on certain individuals to teach them a lesson. That theology is not found in the Bible. He simply instructed them to continue in prayer and fasting in order to fight spiritual battles.

No battle will ever be too great for any Christian, because when we are co-laborers with the God of the universe, it's guaranteed we will always triumph. As 2 Corinthians 2:14 says, "Thanks be to God, who always leads us in triumphal procession in Christ and through us spreads everywhere the fragrance of the knowledge of him."

Reflection Questions

1. Are you co-laboring with God, or are you stuck in the mode of degrading yourself, doubting your abilities, expecting little, and giving even less?
2. How often are you interceding for the lives of those around you?
3. How might you be fighting spiritual battles, and are you praying and fasting to triumph?

CHAPTER 8

Jumping from
the Comfort Zone

CHAPTER 8:
JUMPING FROM THE COMFORT ZONE

*The most common commodity in this country
is unrealized potential.*
— Calvin Coolidge

Choosing to live a life of significance and going up against the odds does not promise a life full of comfort. We can all readily admit that our preferences lean toward comfort and security. Personally, I'd like nothing more than to have a few million dollars in the bank and not have to think about earning my next paycheck. I'd like nothing better than to know the exact day that Jesus is coming back.

Building Character

Jesus, however, is much more interested in building our character than making us comfortable. Choosing to move out of our comfort zones is difficult.

Nehemiah faithfully moved far, far away from his comfort zone. Once he arrived in Jerusalem he became a spokesperson, a construction boss, and a military leader. Just when he thought he'd been stretched to the limit, a new problem popped up. He learned his fellow countrymen had been cheating and defrauding one another.

> Now the men and their wives raised a great outcry against their fellow Jews. Some were saying, "We and our sons and daughters are numerous; in order for us to eat and stay alive, we must get grain."
>
> Others were saying, "We are mortgaging our fields, our vineyards and our homes to get grain during the famine."
>
> Still others were saying, "We have had to borrow money to pay the king's tax on our fields and vineyards. Although we are of the same flesh and blood as our fellow Jews and though our children are as good as theirs, yet we have to subject our sons and daughters to slavery. Some of our daughters have already been enslaved, but we are powerless, because our fields and our vineyards belong to others." (Nehemiah 5:1–5)

Challenging Times

I find it interesting that this account from a time in history more than 3,000 years ago reads like today's news. The economy is faltering, people are out of work, homes are in foreclosure, and people are crying out about being treated unfairly. All this damage is because others are greedy for profit. We live in tough, challenging times, just as they did in Jerusalem during Nehemiah's day.

When this news comes to Nehemiah's attention, what is his reaction?

"Listen folks, I'd like to help you, but I've got enough problems already. I'm trying to rebuild the city wall, which is a near-impossible task. I've organized workers and then I organized an army. Meanwhile, there are enemies out there threatening to kill me. Your financial problems are not my main priority. That's someone else's concern, not mine. Excuse me now while I get back to building the wall."

No one could have blamed him if this had been his reaction. In fact, that would have been the natural response for many of us. We learn in verse 6 of chapter 5 that that was not Nehemiah's answer. On the contrary, he said, "When I heard their outcry and these charges, I was very angry."

Nehemiah's Response

Nehemiah was shocked to learn that the people of Judah were cheating one another, and as their leader, he knew he must intervene.

I pondered [the outcry and charges] in my mind and then accused the nobles and officials. I told them, "You are charging your own people interest!" So I called together a large meeting to deal with them and said: "As far as possible, we have bought back our fellow Jews who were sold to the Gentiles. Now you are selling your own people, only for them to be sold back to us!" They kept quiet, because they could find nothing to say.

So I continued, "What you are doing is not right. Shouldn't you walk in the fear of our God to avoid the reproach of our Gentile enemies? I and my brothers and my men are also lending the people money and grain. But let us stop charging interest! Give back to them immediately their fields, vineyards, olive groves and houses, and also the interest you are charging

them – one percent of the money, grain, new wine and olive oil."
(Nehemiah 5:7–11)

Nehemiah called a meeting and proceeded (in today's vernacular) to
read them the riot act. Point by point, without reservation, he listed their
wrongdoing. Then he took it a step further and demanded restoration to
those who had been cheated. As can be imagined, this would not have made
him the most popular person.

It would be like if I accused the U.S. lending institutions and finance
houses of cheating and robbing people and demanded that they make
it right. I don't think they'd be too happy. I probably wouldn't receive an
invitation to come to the head office to discuss the matter further!

Because Nehemiah was co-laboring with God and because he was
confident of his position, he had the boldness to speak the truth and follow
it up with action. At this point, not only was Nehemiah known as the wall-
builder but he single-handedly changed the entire financial system. He
changed the moral compass of his society. This is an area he probably never
even dreamed of being involved in when he set out from Shushan.

The same can be said for each one of us in our walk with God. When
we are yielded to Him and when we are faithfully following Him, He will
take our small beginnings and cause them to have a bigger impact than we
ever could have imagined. God can accomplish more with our lives than we
ever could have in our own strength.

A Higher Purpose

When we think of how prevalent greed and corruption was in Judah
at this time, why didn't Nehemiah succumb to the temptation to enter in?
How easy it would have been for him. After all, he was the man in charge.
He stood to make a small fortune had he followed the existing patterns of
corruption. But Nehemiah lived for a higher purpose.

In spite of the fact that he had been appointed governor, he did not
even eat the food allotted to him through the governor's office.

But the earlier governors – those preceding me – placed a
heavy burden on the people and took forty shekels of silver from
them in addition to food and wine. Their assistants also lorded it
over the people. But out of reverence for God I did not act like that.

Instead, I devoted myself to the work on this wall. All my men
were assembled there for the work; we did not acquire any land.
(Nehemiah 5:15–16)

Here we learn that those who preceded him not only ate the food allotted to them but also required a tax from the people, which added an additional financial burden. Because Nehemiah revered God, he refused to lower himself to that type of behavior. He lived for a higher purpose.

Who was Nehemiah working for? Clearly, he was working for God. At the end of the day, all he really cared about was what God thought about him. He wasn't building the wall to win a popularity contest. He wasn't building the wall because he enjoyed bossing people around. He wasn't building the wall to get rich or to boost his self-esteem. He only cared what God thought about him.

Nehemiah gives each one of us an amazing pattern to follow. Are we choosing to live for His purpose regardless of the circumstances, or are we taking the easy path?

Asking Hard Questions

When we choose to live following God's purposes, we will live significantly. We will make a difference in the lives of those around us. I often like to ask people the following questions:
- Is the world a better place this year because you are here?
- Is the world better off because you exist?
- Would it have made a difference if you had died last year?
- Would it have made a difference to your community if you were not here this year?
- Would it have made a difference to your coworkers?
- Would it have impacted the lives of your friends or anyone if you were not here?

I ask myself these questions often. Yes, of course, my family would miss me. But beyond that, is my presence making a difference in the lives of others? Am I an encouragement to those with whom I come in contact? Am I helping raise others to a higher level spiritually?

It's easy to say, "One day when I have more money, I will do more. One day when I have more time... One day when I've been a Christian longer... One day when I know the Bible better and have more confidence... I'll reach out then and have an impact on the lives of others."

If we believe those lies, we'll wake up as a seventy – or eighty-year-old man or woman and still not have made a difference in the lives of others. If we're not making a difference now, today, this year, then the chance of it bursting to action next year is highly improbable.

"Give Me Compassion"

Years ago, I worked in children's church with the nine-to-twelve-year-old age group of approximately 300 boys and girls. When you are teaching 300 children at once, it's difficult to interact intimately with any of them. Each week when they arrived, we attempted to give them a good time and sound teaching. But then they left.

One day I realized I had no real compassion for those children. I went before the Lord and begged, "Give me compassion." I asked Him to give me the heart to reach these children and for a deep compassion for their souls. I knew if they were to be reached, I needed a change of heart. Nothing happened instantaneously; however, as the weeks and months passed, I began to weep and pray for these little ones that I was privileged to teach. Things began to change.

Now, years later, when I happen to come across one of these former students, they share with me the things they remember learning during those years. I had no idea the measure of the impact at the time, but God knew and intervened. There may be people in that group who are now on their way to heaven because of the teachings in that class. What started with a small beginning grew to have a big impact.

The Trap of Luxury and Ease

All of us are guilty of settling back into our areas of comfort and being reluctant to move. Everything is going fine, so why rock the boat? Luxury and ease can be a deceptive trap.

I've experienced amazing blessings from God. A few years ago I saved up enough air miles to fly first class between London and America. It was incredible! My wife, Daniela, and our daughter Jordan were with me. The airline gave us a full set of pajamas. We ate dinner at a table and slept in a bed! It was hard to believe we were on the same plane that we usually fly where my seat makes me feel like I'm wearing a shirt that's two sizes too small!

The flight was amazing, and we praise God every day for His goodness and His abundant favor in our lives. As wonderful as a first-class way of life may appear to be, I wouldn't trade my present life and my relationship with God for any luxuries, especially if it lulled me into a state of self-sufficiency or if it distracted me from having a heart after God. Nothing is worth the price of becoming complacent and no longer sensing the need for God.

Many people wonder if Christians can have wealth and still be dependent on God. Absolutely they can! The secret comes in being a river and not a dam. Those types of people know how to keep the flow of blessings going out into the world around them. The lowest form of blessing is to be *blessed*; the highest form is to *be a blessing*.

George Mueller's Desire

George Mueller is most known for his ministry of working with orphaned children. It's interesting, however, that this ministry was his secondary objective. What George desired first and foremost was to have a work that would give visible proof that God hears and answers prayer. Sure, his heart went out to the many ragged children running wild in the streets, but that was not the main reason he started an orphanage.

George Muller was adamant about choosing to live in a way that was totally dependent upon God. Throughout the years of his work, he never sent out appeal letters nor did he ever announce the needs of his orphanages. It was never his plan to slip into a life of comfort where his ear might be dulled to God's voice.

Because of his childlike faith, God showed up in the most miraculous ways, not just once or twice, but on a daily basis. George Mueller gave God room to do something.

Wanting to Be Used

After they have gone on a mission trip, I've never heard anyone say, "The trip was okay, I guess, but I didn't really experience anything. I'm just glad to get home and back to my own life." On the contrary, those who return from giving to others, because they have chosen and positioned themselves to be used by God, return with softened hearts. They are forever changed.

You don't need to travel to a distant land to be used by God; you just have to open your heart and look around.

A life devoted to God will look different from other lives. Nehemiah left his life of comfort and ease and became totally devoted to God and His purpose. As a result, the entire society of Judah was transformed. People viewed one another in a new light. They honored one another and treated one another fairly. They began to honor God in a way that they had not done for many years.

When we move from our comfort zone and fully dedicate our lives to Him, we will walk into a room and sense that someone has a need. We'll know who needs prayer and who needs a word of encouragement. As Isaiah 50:4 tells us, "The Sovereign Lord has given me a well-instructed tongue, to know the word that sustains the weary. He wakens me morning by morning, wakens my ear to listen like one being instructed."

No longer will we hang back or be unsure or hesitant. We will want to be used; we will want to speak that word to the weary. In my own life, I want to be constantly asking God, "What can I do for You? Where can I serve You? How can I impact the people around me?"

I don't ever want God to leave me where I am; I want to be thrust out of my comfort zone.

Reflection Questions

1. Are you living for a higher purpose or just trying to get through the day?
2. Do you work harder at trying to be safe and secure than you do at following God's leading? In what area have you become not just comfortable, but complacent?
3. In what areas can you step out of your comfort zone and choose to make a difference in your world?

CHAPTER 9
Discovering
Your Identity

CHAPTER 9:
DISCOVERING YOUR IDENTITY

Whether you believe you can, or you can't, you are right.
– Henry Ford

In a number of places throughout the Bible we find lists of genealogies. For most of us, they are not much more than boring reading. God, however, has a reason for each and every one of them.

One such list appears in chapter 7 of the book of Nehemiah.

A Genealogy's Purpose

As we have learned about Nehemiah, everything he accomplished in his life was due to following God's guidance and direction. In the preceding chapters we've seen how Nehemiah brought about the rebuilding of the wall, which at the first appeared to be an impossible task.

Now the wall was completed. It had been completed in the span of a mere fifty-two days. But now what? God had that part covered, too. Nehemiah had followed God's guidance, and now God put the idea for a genealogy in his heart.

> So my God put it into my heart to assemble the nobles, the officials and the common people for registration by families. I found the genealogical record of those who had been the first to return. This is what I found written there:
>
> These are the people of the province who came up from the captivity of the exiles whom Nebuchadnezzar king of Babylon had taken captive (they returned to Jerusalem and Judah, each to his own town, in company with Zerubbabel, Joshua, Nehemiah, Azariah, Raamiah, Nahamani, Mordecai, Bilshan, Mispereth, Bigvai, Nehum and Baanah). (Nehemiah 7:5–7)

The Letdown Feeling

Have you ever been involved in a momentous event? Perhaps it was a graduation with finals to study for or maybe it was a big wedding where the details seemed to multiply with each passing day or maybe it was a marathon where you trained for weeks prior. Afterward, did you experience a feeling of being letdown?

When we're pumped up with exertion and expending extra energy, our adrenalin output is heightened. This causes numerous chemical changes after which some people are prone to slip into depression during *letdown* times.

This very thing happened to the prophet Elijah. In the account recorded in 1 Kings 18 and 19, we see this courageous prophet issuing a bold challenge to the prophets who served the god of Baal. Elijah called down fire from heaven and then proceeded to kill all of the false prophets. In anyone's estimation, that had to have been a good day.

Only a short time later, however, Elijah is struggling with depression and entertaining thoughts of suicide. "When he came to Beersheba in Judah, he left his servant there, while he himself went a day's journey into the wilderness. He came to a broom bush, sat down under it and prayed that he might die. 'I have had enough, LORD,' he said. 'Take my life; I am no better than my ancestors.'" (1 Kings 19:3–4)

What an amazing contrast from one day to the next. In the course of a day, Elijah forgot who he was and Whom he served. If this has ever happened to you, you now know you're not alone.

Human tendency to experience letdown may have been part of the reason why God put it in Nehemiah's heart to present the genealogy to the people. Everyday life had to resume after the wall was completed. There was a danger that during this letdown time, the people could have reverted to their old pattern of forgetting God. The genealogy would serve to remind them of who they were, Whom they served, and the strength of their heritage. Many times we as Christians forget who we are and the heritage that we have through Jesus' death on the cross.

Self-Image Built on Lies

For others, it's not a matter of forgetting; it's a matter of never having known in the first place. Some people's self-images have been built on a foundation of lies from the enemy, which has robbed them of accomplishing God's purpose for their lives. The lies of the enemy can rob each one of us of our true identity in God.

We serve a mighty and powerful God, the Creator of the entire universe. Scripture tells us that the same Spirit that raised Jesus from the dead dwells in each one of us. (Romans 8:11). If that is true, and it is, then shouldn't our lives be extraordinary? I believe the only reason why we live ordinary lives is because we've believed lies. We've been deceived into believing that we are powerless.

A Self-Image Problem

Consider this self-image problem. On a high craggy mountain peak, a mother eagle had built her nest and laid four eggs. One day an earthquake rocked the mountain, causing one of the eggs to roll down the mountain into a chicken farm in the valley below. A mother hen found the egg and nurtured it by keeping it warm and safe. Soon the egg hatched and a beautiful eagle was born. But because the eagle grew up with the chickens, he believed himself to be nothing more than a chicken. The eagle loved his home and family, but his spirit cried out for more.

One day the eagle looked up to the skies and saw a group of mighty eagles soaring up toward the mountain peak. "Oh," the eagle cried. "I wish I could soar like those birds." The chickens all laughed at this remark. "You can't soar with those birds. You're a chicken and chickens can't soar."

The eagle continued gazing at the eagles above, dreaming that he could be with them. Each time the eagle let his dreams be known, he was told it was impossible. The eagle was taught a lie and believed it. The eagle, eventually, stopped dreaming and became satisfied living his life as a chicken. Finally, after a long life as a chicken, the eagle died, never knowing his true destiny.

We are fueled in our spirits by the same fuel source that empowered Jesus to shake off the chains of death and escape the confines of hell; yet our lives, for the most part, may look like any other person living on the earth. We must be taught about our heritage; we must be taught about the mighty God we serve. We have to know we are eagles before we will believe that we can soar.

Our Beliefs About God

Our beliefs about God will directly affect our inner beliefs about ourselves. If we see God as a big bully up in the sky, uncaring and unfeeling, waiting to smack down those who are going the wrong way, then we will forever condemn ourselves for every wrongdoing.

If I were to hear a rumor that someone had accused my wife of being a prostitute, I would be filled with anger. I would want to find the perpetrator of that vicious lie and deal with that individual to set him or her straight. It would be unthinkable to me that anyone could say such a horrible thing about such a wonderful woman. And yet, I constantly hear people saying things about my loving God that absolutely are not true. They accuse God of acts that are the result of a ruthless enemy at large in a fallen world.

We serve a God of love and mercy who made the ultimate sacrifice by giving His own Son to die for us. He is filled with compassion, and the Bible says He does not condemn us. (Romans 8:1; John 3:17).

Who are we that God should love us so much? That's what we must come to know. We are His chosen ones; we are His workmanship (masterpiece); we are His children; we are His beloved. He loves us so much that Jesus calls us His friends.

Doing Exploits for God

The person who is confused about his or her identity will never accomplish what God designed him or her to do. The person who listens to the lies of the enemy will continue to lead an ordinary life, never moving into the higher calling of Father God. God has great plans for each and every one of His children. "For I know the thoughts that I think toward you, saith the LORD, thoughts of peace, and not of evil, to give you an expected end" (Jeremiah 29:11).

Daniel 11:32 KJV says, "The people that do know their God shall be strong, and do exploits." Notice that *knowing* God comes before doing exploits. It becomes obvious as we examine the life of Nehemiah that he knew his God intimately. As a result, he knew who he was in God and he did mighty exploits.

Authority

When we know who we are in God, we will understand that we have authority to stand against the enemy. Jesus referred to this authority when He said, "I have given you authority to trample on snakes and scorpions and to overcome all the power of the enemy; nothing will harm you" (Luke 10:19).

If a gunfight broke out in a neighborhood over a bad drug deal and the police arrived, they would dive right into the danger. They would do that at the same time the civilians ran for cover. One group would be going in. One group would be going out.

What makes the difference? *Authority.* The police officers have authority. They are *authorized* to move in and route the enemy. They also understand their purpose, what they are trained for. If there is crime, the police run in. If there is fire, firemen run in. In the same way, where there is darkness, Christians should be running in and shining the light of God. That's what we've been made for.

We've been given authority to route the enemy of God. We've been given power to overcome *all* the power of the enemy. A person in power will not sit idly by and accept the status quo. When we know who we are in God, we will begin to lead extraordinary lives that make a difference in the world around us. When I know my authority, I can't sit idly by when someone who is suffering needs prayer or when a discouraged person needs an encouraging word or when a family is in financial need and I have the means to help. When marriages are falling apart, I am moved to make a difference.

When I was in India, I was praying for people after one service. A woman came up who had leprosy in her feet. That was not the moment for me to begin wondering if my God is in the healing business. That was not the moment for me to wonder if I really did have God's authority working in my life. I had to know beyond a doubt, since I not only laid hands on her feet but continued to lay hands on everyone after her. I knew who I was in God. I knew my God, and I knew Him to be trustworthy and faithful. I believed He would take care of the matter.

Know the Difference

Repeatedly throughout the Scriptures God lets us know who we are, what we have in Him, and what He is to us. When we renew our minds to these promises, the devil has no entrance. He may come to you with lies, telling you that you're a mistake, that you'll never amount to anything, that you're a failure, that you always mess things up, or that God has no time for you. But once truth is deeply embedded in your heart and mind, you will know the difference between God's truth and Satan's lies.

People who work in the banking system are taught to detect a counterfeit bill by studying bills that are genuine. Once they are thoroughly trained in what the real deal looks like, they are able to detect the counterfeit. The same holds true with our knowledge about God's love for us. Once you've experienced the genuine article, the lies of the enemy will never again trip you up.

Our Names Are Sealed

Nehemiah was well aware that his fellow countrymen had forgotten who they were. They had forgotten what a mighty God they served. They had forgotten that they were a chosen race of people. Once each person saw their names written in that genealogy book, and heard their name being called out as the list was read, they received a fresh revelation of who they were. Those who were not of the proper lineage were separated out.

In the same way, when we accept Jesus as Lord and Savior and become His child, our names are written in the Lamb's book of life (Philippians 4:3; Revelation 20:15). He cares so much about each one of us that He has sealed our commitment to Him by writing our names in His book.

Perhaps you've been struggling with the question of who you are. Maybe you wonder in the scheme of the world if you even matter.

The answer is yes, you *do* matter. You matter a great deal to your heavenly Father. He wants to demonstrate not only His love to you, but His power in your life. You were designed to do amazing exploits.

We often value people according to the wages they earn. In a worldly sense, someone who earns $800 an hour is worth more than someone who earns $5. In the same way, someone with a net worth of $1 billion is viewed as being worth more than someone who lives in debt.

Have you ever stopped to consider your worth? If I told you that you were worth $1 billion dollars, would that change how you felt about yourself? If you were in a hostage situation and someone was willing to pay $2 billion for your release, would that change the way you carry yourself?

The truth is you are so valuable that God felt that you were worth the price of His Son's life. You are so precious that Jesus endured a horrific marring and beating on your account.

Reflection Questions

1. In what ways have you been listening to the chicken talk, the chicken expectations, and the chicken thinking?
2. In what ways can you cease the chicken lifestyle and soar as the eagle you were meant to be?

The Power of Rest

CHAPTER 10: THE POWER OF REST

God, you have made us for yourself, and our hearts are restless till they find their rest in you.
– Augustine

Once the walls surrounding the city of Jerusalem were completed and the list compiled, it was a time for celebration, rejoicing, and rest. The people gathered together in the "square by the Water Gate" (Nehemiah 8:1). Ezra the scribe and teacher was asked to bring out the writings of Moses to be read aloud.

For the occasion, a large wooden platform was constructed upon which Ezra stood so the crowd could see and hear him. He read the Word of God from early morning till noon. The people's hearts were touched and moved by the Spirit of God and they began to weep.

One of the reasons the Jewish people were taken into exile was because they had neglected to stay true to God's instructions in His Word. Hearing these anointed words convicted their hearts of their sins, and the sins of their fathers before them, and caused them to bow down and worship God.

The Word was not only read aloud, but the Levites were called upon to *explain* the meaning to the people. "They read from the Book of the Law of God, making it clear and giving the meaning so that the people understood what was being read" (Nehemiah 8:8). Once the commands of God were brought to their remembrance, it caused hearts to be repentant, and they confessed their sins before God.

Sabbath Rest

Next, Nehemiah instructed the people regarding the celebration of the Feast of Tabernacles, which was instigated by Moses. As explained in Leviticus 23, the feast week was a time of rest and rejoicing. On the first day and on the eighth day, they were not to do any work. "So beginning with the fifteenth day of the seventh month, after you have gathered the crops of the land, celebrate the festival to the LORD for seven days; the first day is a day of sabbath rest, and the eighth day also is a day of sabbath rest" (Leviticus 23:39).

We see throughout Scripture that our God is a God of rest. He himself rested after the creation of the universe and He then instructed the children of Israel to observe one day of rest every week. Even as they were trekking through the wilderness, feasting on manna each day, they were never allowed to gather manna on the Sabbath day. Those who disobeyed found out that manna gathered on the Sabbath quickly spoiled.

Additionally, God designed sabbatical years for the land itself to rest. Once they arrived in the land of Canaan, the Promised Land, God instructed them to work the land and harvest crops. Every seventh year, however, the land was to lie fallow or untilled.

Keeping of the Sabbath and the sabbatical year was largely ignored by Israel, which, in part, led to their downfall. Their misunderstanding of rest got them into a great deal of trouble. The same can be said for us today. The idea of rest, apart from God, can cause multiple problems in our lives. In our confusion, we rest from things that require our constant vigilance; yet, we drive ourselves relentlessly with busyness that has no eternal value.

Wrong Kind of Rest

What is God's rest, and how can we know the difference between that and improper rest? We see in Nehemiah 9 that in the reading of God's Word, the Israelites were able review their past history. In that review, an amazing truth about rest appears in verse 28: "But as soon as they were at rest, they again did what was evil in your sight. Then you abandoned them to the hand of their enemies so that they ruled over them."

This is startling. It appears to be a contradiction. Didn't God want them to rest? Didn't He give them Sabbath days and feasts in which to rest? Why then was it during rest that they committed so much evil that God abandoned them to their enemies?

The rest that is referred to in this verse tells us that they rested from serving God, knowing God, and observing God's commandments. It's not referring to physical rest.

All of us love to go on vacation and get away from it all. Vacations can be a time of rest and refreshment for our bodies, minds, and emotions. Likewise, a day off work or the weekends or holidays can provide rest. All of us need to give our bodies proper times of rest, so we can recuperate from the demands and stresses of everyday life. Even one good night's sleep can change our temperament and attitudes.

Individuals who drive themselves, failing to incorporate proper rest into their schedules, may pay the price in health issues later on, such as high blood pressure, heart problems, or ulcers. God created our bodies to require, and benefit from, physical rest.

God does not, however, want us to take a rest from serving Him nor to rest from the disciplines of a Christ-centered life. When we rest from prayer; from depending on God; from stretching, reaching, and building up our spiritual side; from accomplishing our purpose in God; this is when we open the door and allow the enemy to enter.

King David's Error in Judgment

An example of the wrong kind of rest can be found in the life of King David. Scripture tells us, "In the spring, at the time when kings go off to war, David sent Joab out with the king's men and the whole Israelite army. They destroyed the Ammonites and besieged Rabbah. But David remained in Jerusalem." (2 Samuel 11:1)

Spring was the time for war, a time to do battle, but David chose to stay home and take a little rest. During his rest, the enemy slipped in with a strong temptation. "One evening David got up from his bed and walked around on the roof of the palace. From the roof he saw a woman bathing. The woman was very beautiful, and David sent someone to find out about her." (2 Samuel 11:2)

A beautiful woman and a man with too much free time on his hands, a man with his guard down, a man who was king over an entire nation, became a combination for disaster.

In the same way, we can never take a rest from battling the enemy of our souls. We are always to be vigilant and on guard. We are to pray constantly. We are to meditate on the Word day and night. It's the moment we think we have it all together and can take a little rest – like King David – that's the moment the enemy can make his entrance and inflict much damage. He does not want you to make a difference in your world.

Resting in God

There is yet another facet of the concept of rest, and that is learning to rest in God; to rest in His promises, and to rest in His care for you. What's the difference between resting on a vacation and resting in God? Resting in the Lord means that you can be in the most difficult circumstances of your life, but you still have an inner peace.

When you face terrible trials in your life, you may have the time and resources to take a wonderful vacation, but you will not be at rest. You cannot rest on your day off when things are falling apart around you, but you can rest in God in any circumstance.

A few years ago, my goal was to cease from toil, struggle, and stress. I wanted to learn to rest in the Lord. It was definitely a learning process. At times I felt I was on top of it, and other times I felt totally overwhelmed. But today I can say that I'm able to rest in God in bigger and more serious difficulties than I ever have before. Now it takes a much bigger challenge to shake me out of my ongoing rest in Him.

A true rest in God ultimately has to do with trusting Him in every situation and circumstance. That rest comes when we truly believe that God's Word means what it says, and we can trust His Word in each and every challenge we come up against.

In fact, failing to rest in God is a sin. In chapter 4 of the book of Hebrews, we learn that an unwillingness to enter into God's rest is an act of disobedience. "Let us, therefore, make every effort to enter that rest, so that no one will perish by following their example of disobedience" (v. 11).

In every facet of Nehemiah's life, we see him resting in God. We see no hint that he ever hesitated, doubted, or questioned God. As Nehemiah faced overwhelming odds against him, he gives us all a sterling example of exactly what it means to enter into the rest of God.

While it's crucial that each of us takes part in physical rest, we are never to rest from (or neglect) the Christian disciplines of prayer, worship, meditation on the Word, or the gathering together with other believers.

Ultimately, rest for Christians in the truest sense of the term means that we are safe and secure in the arms of the One who loves us deeply and cares for us intently. As 1 Peter 5:7 says, "Cast all your anxiety on him because he cares for you."

Reflection Questions

1. When was the last time God's Word moved your heart? How did you respond?
2. Have you ever rested from God and the Christian disciplines? What was the result?
3. Explain in your own words how failing to rest in God is an act of disobedience.
4. What can you do today to begin resting more in God? Be specific.

CHAPTER 11
Your Epic Story of Significance

CHAPTER 11:
YOUR EPIC STORY OF SIGNIFICANCE

The only thing necessary for the triumph of evil
is for good men to do nothing.
– Edmund Burke

We've seen the amazing epic story of the life of Nehemiah and how he changed history forever. He became a history maker.

Encouraging or Discouraging

This account can be a great inspiration for us today. For some people, however, such stories of incredible, amazing accomplishments have the opposite effect. Instead of being an inspiration to them, they feel discouraged and disappointed. They may even condemn themselves. They look at their own lives and wonder, *"How can I ever get to that place? The more I read about how incredible certain people are, the more I feel like a loser."*

Can you relate? Sometimes I feel that way too. I start thinking – *I just don't think I can get there.* I start comparing myself to others and feel like quitting because I can't imagine being where they are.

Those of us who struggle in this way do so because we compare where we're starting to where the other person is finishing. We have to remember that epic stories, events, and people, such as Nehemiah, all began with something or someone very ordinary.

An Errand Boy

One day a young shepherd was called in from the fields, and his father told him to take food to the army of Israel where his older brothers were serving.

Now Jesse said to his son David, "Take this ephah of roasted grain and these ten loaves of bread for your brothers and hurry to their camp. Take along these ten cheeses to the commander of their unit. See how your brothers are and bring back some assurance from them. They are with Saul and all the men of Israel in the Valley of Elah, fighting against the Philistines." (1 Samuel 17:17–19)

At this stage of David's life, he was nothing more than an errand boy. In obedience to his father, he left the sheep and made his delivery. It never occurred to him that before the day was out he would become a national hero. It was an ordinary day, and David was doing ordinary things. He wasn't set on becoming famous.

Frederick Smith and FedEx

Frederick W. Smith wasn't on his way to make a multimillion dollar business when he first wrote a college paper in the 1960s, outlining the need for an overnight delivery system in the United States. The idea incubated in his head for a number of years before he started a company, which he called Federal Express. On the first night of continuous operation in 1973, 389 Federal Express employees and 14 jets delivered 186 packages overnight to 25 U.S. cities. It was the birth of the modern air/ground express business.

Today, FedEx is a worldwide business, the largest of its industry. Its staff numbers more than a quarter of a million employees with 1,500 offices globally. But it began on an ordinary day in an ordinary way for a student named Frederick Smith, long before anyone dreamed of FedEx becoming a household word.

Google

Most of us work in an environment that utilizes a computer server for the business. When there are problems with the server, usually the business operations are shut down until the problems are solved.

Google, the largest search engine in the world, maintains more than 1.7 million servers. How could one entity keep maintenance going for that many servers? It's mind-boggling. Quite obviously, the company didn't begin with that many servers. It grew from a few to many in a progression. It required a first step.

Take the First Step

Don't let the epic stories of others make your dream, your vision, appear small and insignificant. Don't let what others have accomplished cause you to lose your belief that you can succeed against the odds. Hold on to your vision, and don't let anything extinguish it. God is beside you to empower you every step of the way. Remember that it all begins by taking that very first step. You take that first step by praying, "Lord, I want my life to count for You. I want my life to be significant. No matter where I go today, show me how heaven can invade earth through me. Show me how I can make a difference."

This is how ordinary lives become epic stories. It happens when we are willing to allow heaven to come to earth through us wherever we go – in a restaurant, on a bus, in class, in a store, at work, in church, at home. God has given us the privilege and the ability to pray down heaven to earth wherever we go. (Matthew 6:10). When this kind of intention becomes a pattern in your life, you soon will be affecting lives around you in a positive way and your epic story will grow.

From One Mile to Thirteen

A few years ago, due to a series of bad food choices, I put on extra weight – forty pounds to be exact. I knew the only way I was going to lose that weight was to start an exercise program. For me, that involves running. Although I have had asthma since childhood, God gave me the desire, courage, and ability to become a record-setting runner in high school. Fast forward a bunch of years. I'd become lax in exercising, and now to get back into the swing of it, I had to take the first step.

At first I could barely run a mile, and I had to take several breaks during that mile because I was so out of shape. Day after day as I ran that mile, I felt like nothing was happening. I could see no results. My fitness level seemed to remain the same, and my weight didn't budge. But I didn't quit; I kept taking those steps.

I like to compare this to an epic life journey, because it captures where many of us are right now. We try taking steps towards significance, but it seems as if we're not making any difference. Don't quit; keep taking those steps.

One day, I was able to run two miles, and then three. By the end of the year, I ran in the Austin Half Marathon. A half marathon is a 13.1-mile course, and this one was considered to be one of the toughest routes in the country because of the hills. Since I had lost weight and was again in shape, I finished in 1 hour and 52 minutes. Those first steps I took on the tarmac seemed so insignificant, but they led me to finish the Austin Half Marathon. The greatest journeys always begin with a single step.

God's Word

Nehemiah's actions brought heaven (God's will) to earth day after day as he met challenge after challenge against incredible odds. Not only did he obey God's directives, he also spoke God's directives and saw amazing changes take place in the circumstances around him. "Don't be afraid of [our enemies]," he told the people. "Remember the Lord, who is great and awesome, and fight for your families, your sons and your daughters, your wives and your homes" (Nehemiah 4:14).

In the same way, when we apply God's Word to our situations here on earth, God's power comes into play. God's power invades earth through His Word. God created the entire universe by His Word; He spoke galaxies into existence by his Word. "Through faith we understand that the worlds were framed by the word of God, so that things which are seen were not made of things which do appear" (Hebrews 11:3).

Each child of God can have an epic story every day as he or she applies God's Word to the situation. You can pray for others using Scripture verses and expect things to change. You can pray over the obstacles and challenges in your life using God's Word, and you can expect things to change. Because God cannot lie, His Word will take precedence over the prevailing circumstances and you will see victory.

You can be up against financial challenges. If you know God's promises for abundance for His children, then that lack has to give way to God's Word because He cannot lie. Once you grasp this concept, life becomes infinitely more exciting because you recognize the power of His Word. You will be bringing heaven to earth because you understand that God's Word overrides your current circumstances.

When you are up against the odds, God's Word can change the odds. He can turn the odds in your favor.

Nehemiah's Example

Nehemiah's journey started on an ordinary day when he heard bad news. He chose to take one step by approaching the king for favor. From there he took the next step and moved out of his comfort zone, traveling all the way from Shushan (in today's Iran) to Judah (in today's Israel). He believed God's Word, he spoke God's Word, and he stood on God's Word. In doing so, all the odds that he was originally up against were turned in his favor.

Nothing happened in Nehemiah's life that is not available to each child of God today. In fact, what was available to Nehemiah is available to us – and more! Since, as we learned in chapter 6, we've been given an even better covenant than the old one.

You can face the odds, you can begin small in an ordinary way, and your life can become an epic story. Dare to believe God for it and get ready for the most exciting time of your life! I believe in you, but more importantly, God believes in you!

Reflection Questions

1. Do heroic stories of others tend more to inspire or discourage you?
2. How have you shortchanged yourself by comparing your journey to others?
3. What step can you take today to move closer to what God is calling you to do?

We ourselves feel that what we are doing is just a drop in the ocean. But the ocean would be less because of that missing drop.
– Mother Teresa

ABOUT THE AUTHOR

Brent Phillips

As a native of South Africa, I studied software engineering at Rand Afrikaans University in Johannesburg and had my own systems engineering company. But I left it all and moved to the United States to work in Christian ministry, becoming ordained in 2006.

Since then, I have had the privilege of ministering internationally as well. In addition, I was an advisor to several companies and served as the CTO for 2nd.MD, a revolutionary company that helps change lives by providing online access to top medical specialists when a second opinion is needed.

From a young age, I have known what it's like to be up against the odds. I experienced abandonment by my father, homelessness, and poverty, and God's provision.

At the age of five, I developed acute asthma and was barely able to walk. I was encouraged when my mother showed me Isaiah 40:31: "But those who hope in the Lord will renew their strength. They will soar on wings like eagles; they will run and not grow weary, they will walk and not be faint." I took the promise literally and repeatedly and unsuccessfully tried out for elementary school track.

Still claiming Isaiah 40:31 in high school, I entered the 1,500 meter tryouts. To the glory of God, I set a school record that stood for twenty years. I experienced many other miracles of God over the years, including recovering from a horrendous auto accident and being able to enter the university without having completed all of the mathematics requirements.

A Desert Time

No one enjoys going through a desert experience, that time where God feels distant and everything seems dry and painful. Usually these times come after great success. After striving and struggling for breakthrough in ministry in Aspen, Colorado things could not have been better, people were passionate about change and church, services were full and God was moving. In midst of all of this we had planned a church-wide mission trip to South Africa and everything was going according to plan until we received news that our new U.S. visa was declined. We had a choice to make: Skip the mission trip and try to rectify the situation or sacrifice "everything" we had worked so hard for, or sell up and move back to South Africa. Knowing the impact this trip would have on countless lives, we sold up and went back to South Africa.

The mission trip was a success in every sense of the word; lives were forever challenged and changed, but now what? We moved around from house to house, with a two-year-old and a two-month-old baby, while I tried to find the "open door." Nothing opened, in fact I felt as if they were dead-bolt locked as well. All the success of ministry in Aspen became a distant memory and our resources were disappearing quickly. It was the first time in my life that I did not have my immediate family around for support, and stress and depression started to set in.

To add gasoline to fire, we were running out of money. After not being able to find work in any capacity, the inevitable happened and I had to face a fear that I never thought I would have to, not being able to provide for my family. Once again, we were down on our knees asking God to rescue us.

God, Our Rock, Our Fortress

The very day that I had no idea how I was going to put food on the table, I received a call from my brother Clint. Not knowing our plight, he told me that he was able to raise money for his new business. He wired $10,000 to my account to start developing the software. It was a day of celebration, but the joy would be challenged. That same week we received the news that we could never come back to the U.S., because I had used up all my visas. It was a deathly blow. Would we ever see our family again and everything we had known for the past nine years?

Back on our knees, but this time, we weren't begging God for our plans to succeed, but submitting our lives to Him. We only wanted to be where He wanted us, and we only wanted to be doing what He wanted us to do. I was finally ready to sacrifice it all, and the sacrifice was "my" ministry. I had so loved preaching, that I had found my identity in it, and this is what needed to be stripped away. My identity needed to be found in God alone, not in my activities, no matter how noble. Success was never to be measured on external factors, but internal – finding our satisfaction, joy and reason for living in God alone. Through this time my wife and I became best friends too!

The next day my mom, while in Houston, was talking to someone about our dilemma and they recommended a lawyer in Houston. We had dealt with countless lawyers and there was no solution. But God! On this particular day, God opened a door that didn't seem to exist. While talking to the lawyer, it came up that my wife is a German citizen and God used this to bring us back to the U.S. We were coming back changed people with different hearts and minds. Broken and surrendered, God had now positioned us for His will and not ours.

2nd.MD

After my brother's little girl suffered a stroke at an early age and their family was going through an awful experience trying to figure out what had actually happened and what the next steps were, 2nd.MD was born. It was a way for anyone with medical questions, conditions, medications or mysteries to speak directly to the top specialists so that what they went through did not have to happen to anyone else. This was the business idea my brother had called about during such a desperate season for us. I returned back to the world of software engineering and thought this was going to be the path for my life. I was an ordained pastor working as a software engineer but I was so grateful to have a job and to be around my family again. Pastoring had become a distant memory and preaching even more so.

Big Opportunities Might Look Small

Life seemed to be amazing. Everything was a reason for celebration. Even a street lamp was beautiful after not having power and water many times in South Africa. It is amazing how quickly "self" wants to pop back up when life stabilizes. We wanted to join a small church like our mountain church in Aspen because thats where we felt comfortable. Once again God would lead and guide so patiently and gently out of our comfort and into His plan.

A friend, Brett Moody, who attended Second Baptist Church in Houston, Texas, and taught a Bible study along with the senior pastor's wife, called one day and asked if I would teach his class for the summer while he was in Aspen. My immediate response was no. It was a response out of insecurity. After going from a season of "success" to a season of such "failure," I wasn't even sure if I was supposed to be in ministry anymore. God would use this experience to seal my call and confidence in Him, no matter the season. After praying, it did not seem as if God had anywhere else for us to go, so I reluctantly and nervously accepted the opportunity, warning my friend that this may reflect badly on him.

I attended another Second Baptist Bible study class where my brother was teaching to simply get an idea of what I was getting myself into, not realizing I would meet the person (Lisa Milne) who is on staff at Second Baptist Church and who God would use to bring me out of obscurity. We nervously joined Second Baptist Church and I began teaching Bible study classes.

Something Is Wrong, But What?

Even though I had nothing to complain about, after a few years, I was becoming increasingly restless. Although I had been given an amazing opportunity as CTO at 2nd.MD, I longed to do something else but could not put my finger on what it was. I had ruled out vocational ministry in my mind, I didn't even entertain it as a choice. I loved teaching the Bible studies, and I couldn't wait for the next opportunity. In fact they couldn't come fast enough. I would sometimes teach 3 times on a weekend and it was never enough. The size of the class did not matter, I taught classes of 30 and classes sometimes of 5, but God's word had never been more delicious and real to me and I couldn't wait to serve it up to everyone who was hungry. After coming from such a dark place and now having been rescued yet again, I wanted to share it with everyone who would listen so that they too could experience the amazing love, grace and power of God in their lives.

A week was too long to wait in order to share this with people. After asking my church for permission, I started a Bible study on Tuesdays in the home of Jeff and Shana Wood. It had 8 hungry people who wanted to know as much as possible, who did not want to live mediocre Christian lives, but to experience God daily. The passion to share the gospel that had taken me to Aspen nearly a decade before began to rise in me once again. I was starting to find my way home. God began restoring what was lost and in a short period he had filled our lives with incredible friends and support, but I still was restless.

The Greatest Job Offer

The Bible study grew almost every week, and after only five months we had grown to over 100 people. It was insane. We were packing out houses. People everywhere. It did not matter where they sat, as long as they could hear God's Word. But we were out of space, what was next?

Every now and then in life you meet someone who just loves you and you can't figure out why. Their genuine belief in you melts away skepticism and breaks down walls that we build in times of hurt and disappointment, that no matter what angle you look from, you can't find an ulterior motive. One day while sitting in Lisa Milne's office talking about my plans, frustrations and the Bible study, she made me the greatest job offer I had ever heard. Lisa said "We can help you reach far more people for Jesus than you can by yourself."

That was it! That was what I had been looking for; it was simply wanting to reach people for Jesus with my life not just on the side. Why couldn't I see that all along? My excuses and fears about returning to vocational ministry melted in an instant in the light of that statement. There was only one answer to that statement, YES! The prodigal preacher was coming home!

Another Lesson In Surrender

After God confirming in prayer with my wife, we nervously started making plans to make this dream a reality. God provided the person to replace me at 2nd.MD and it seemed as if all was in order. About a month before I started, two men visited my Bible study, not knowing that I was going on staff at Second Baptist Church, they were searching for a senior pastor at another church, and they offered me the job. They were exceptionally kind and laid out the benefits.

I would be a senior pastor at 34, I would live in a beautiful parsonage with many other benefits. My "pastoral" resume would suddenly have something worth noting. I would be the "big dog" at the helm. On paper, it was truly an amazing offer compared to the "unknown" position at Second Baptist where preaching was not even on the table. For someone who loves preaching, it would seem the choice was obvious. To make the offer even more apparent, due to financial reasons, we would have to move into a small apartment in order to take the job at Second Baptist. I have made many mistakes in my life, and will make many again, but looking back on this decision, I can smile from ear to ear that I finally made a decision based on God's plan and nothing else.

It was a decision based on surrender. I chose the place where I could be surrendered, where I could once again lay down my ambition on the altar but this time with joy. My pastor (Steve Woodrow) in Aspen told me once, "It is far more important who you do ministry with, than where you do ministry." I now have the privilege of being in vocational ministry with the amazing people at Second Baptist who have been led so faithfully by our beloved pastor, Dr. Ed Young. For possibly the first time in my life, I had no preconceived ideas on what and how God should use me. I didn't require anything and I had no demands, I just wanted to be used by God to see people come to know Jesus in the way He wanted to do it… and we loved our apartment!

When It Rains, It Pours

In life, you cannot control whether or not it rains, but you can choose to put on a coat, boots and dance in the rain. In a period of two months, my cousin (Many Gold) was killed by a drunk driver, another cousin (Tammy Andrassy) lost their baby a week before full term, and one of my best friends and father-mentor

(Stacy Taylor) died of a heart attack. Compounded by many other tests and trials it seemed as if all hell had broken loose. We were no stranger to death and loss, having lost so many people in the past, but the pain is always brand new.

During these times there are two paths you can take: To become bitter because of the unknown reasons why or to press in on what we do know. I don't know why all these things have happened, but what I do know is God is good.

I have chosen to concentrate on what I do understand and not on what I don't, on what God has revealed and not what He hasn't. When all hell breaks loose, it means you are doing something good, and the best news is… hell can't prevail.

At the same time of these massive challenges, we have seen massive impact. The Bible study I was teaching out grew the homes where we were meeting. We started meeting in a large room at Second Baptist Church where attendance doubled and doubled and doubled. At a recent special event for the Bible study, we had over 1,100 people attend with over 8 different denominations in the same room and many people surrendering their lives to God. We are only at the beginning of what God is about to do. If the world's singers and rappers can fill stadiums based on garbage, we can overfill stadiums with people who are desperate to hear about truth.

What Is Happening Now?

God continues to melt mountains and fill in valleys on our behalf. This book is dedicated to bringing hope, that no matter what you are facing, no matter what you are going through, God can make a way, God can turn it around and God loves you!

THANK YOU!

I pray that you have been greatly encouraged by God's Word and that the time you have spent reading this book has planted seeds in your heart that will bear much fruit in your life. You were made to do great things with God.

– Brent

To contact Brent Phillips for your next event:

NeverJustExist

1415 South Voss #110-399
Houston, TX 77057

Phone: 713-367-1859
Email: contact@neverjustexist.com
Web: www.neverjustexist.com
Twitter: brentgphillips
Facebook: neverjustexist

11719367R00080

Made in the USA
San Bernardino, CA
27 May 2014